MW01706864

Rufie: A Political Scrapbook

Edited by Philip Bean and Gene Nassar

In commemoration of the gift of the scrapbooks from Angela Elefante
to the Utica Public Library at a reception at the Library on November 15, 2009

Published by the Ethnic Heritage Studies Center
Utica College

Distributed by Syracuse University Press

Printed in the United States of America

ISBN 978-0-9660363-6-7

Preface

by Eugene Paul Nassar

Over the years, Angela Elefante kept voluminous scrapbooks of clippings and articles, both positive and negative, about her legendary father. There is not much correspondence in these scrapbooks, because Rufus Elefante never cared to hold public office, preferring the private sphere of political power, especially during his years of ascendancy, roughly 1928-58. Angela recently turned over copies of these scrapbooks to Phil Bean and me, and together we have made the selections presented in this volume, with all the text the work of Phil. The selections were made primarily to maintain reader interest and avoid repetition and monotony. There is here not more than a small fraction of the scrapbook items. Thus, as the scrapbooks over the years covered the newspaper articles on, say, the Utica Water Board, there was the inevitable tedious repetition along with the occasional fireworks, so that we have edited and included a few items of interest and leave it to a later scholar to research the full collection on the given issue. To that end, Angela has agreed to donate the scrapbooks and copies of the full archival collection to the Utica Public Library.

The clippings from the Utica Gannett newspapers are often the product of the necessarily tense relationship between government and the press, though there are here included some very lively and informative pieces written by David Beetle, Ed Byrne, Bill Lohden, Mike Woods, Richard Benedetto, Marj Patrick, William Monopoli, Laurence Paul, Tony Vella, Mason Taylor, and others. And though Angela might want to disagree somewhat, it seems to me that Rufie has had some good scholarly work done about him, by, say, Jack Germond, Stuart Witt, Paul Williams, Dennis Burek, Warren Moscow, Alan Ehrenhalt, Alexander Thomas, Warren Weaver, and, to be sure, Phil Bean (all of which Angela has in the scrapbooks). Excerpts from some of these articles are herein included. This volume and the Elefante collection at the Utica Public Library will make subsequent research into the Rufie era a good deal easier for others.

What is sadly fast disappearing is the rich anecdotal material that can only be supplied by people who knew Rufus Elefante, worked for and interacted with him. Stories about Rufie and his operatives are legion, and endlessly retold; some are certainly exaggerated and apocryphal. It is probably too late to sort through them. As with any iconic political "boss," all we can do is listen to them, enjoy them, and then put them up against what meager historical documentation we have.

What I can do here at least is to relate what I know for sure of Rufie's impact on *my* family. My father and mother were immigrants from Lebanon in 1912, and my father worked all of his life as a foreman in a plaster mill on Broad Street. My two brothers were students at Syracuse University on the GI Bill after WWII. No one in the family knew—or ever knew—Rufus Elefante at all. But my brother Mike was looking for work after graduating from Syracuse U. in 1949, and Rufie's local committeeman for our 700 block of Lansing Street offered Mike an entry level job as a caseworker at the Department of Welfare, from which Mike later rose to be the Commissioner of Welfare.

In the sixties, after I had the PhD and was teaching first at Hamilton College and then at Utica College, I was approached by a lawyer friend to tell me he had a message from Rufie. I had never met Rufus Elefante, but the message asked if I was interested in running for the Utica School Board, and if I was, Rufie would support me. I was so heavily into teaching and research that I gratefully declined, but never forgot. And then at that time, my brother Fred, a Harvard lawyer and as bright and as perceptive a man as there was, said to me that Rufie was so much brighter and so far ahead of anyone else in local politics that there was just no contest.

But these are just my stories among so many from so many others. Just one example of why Rufie will not be easily forgotten.

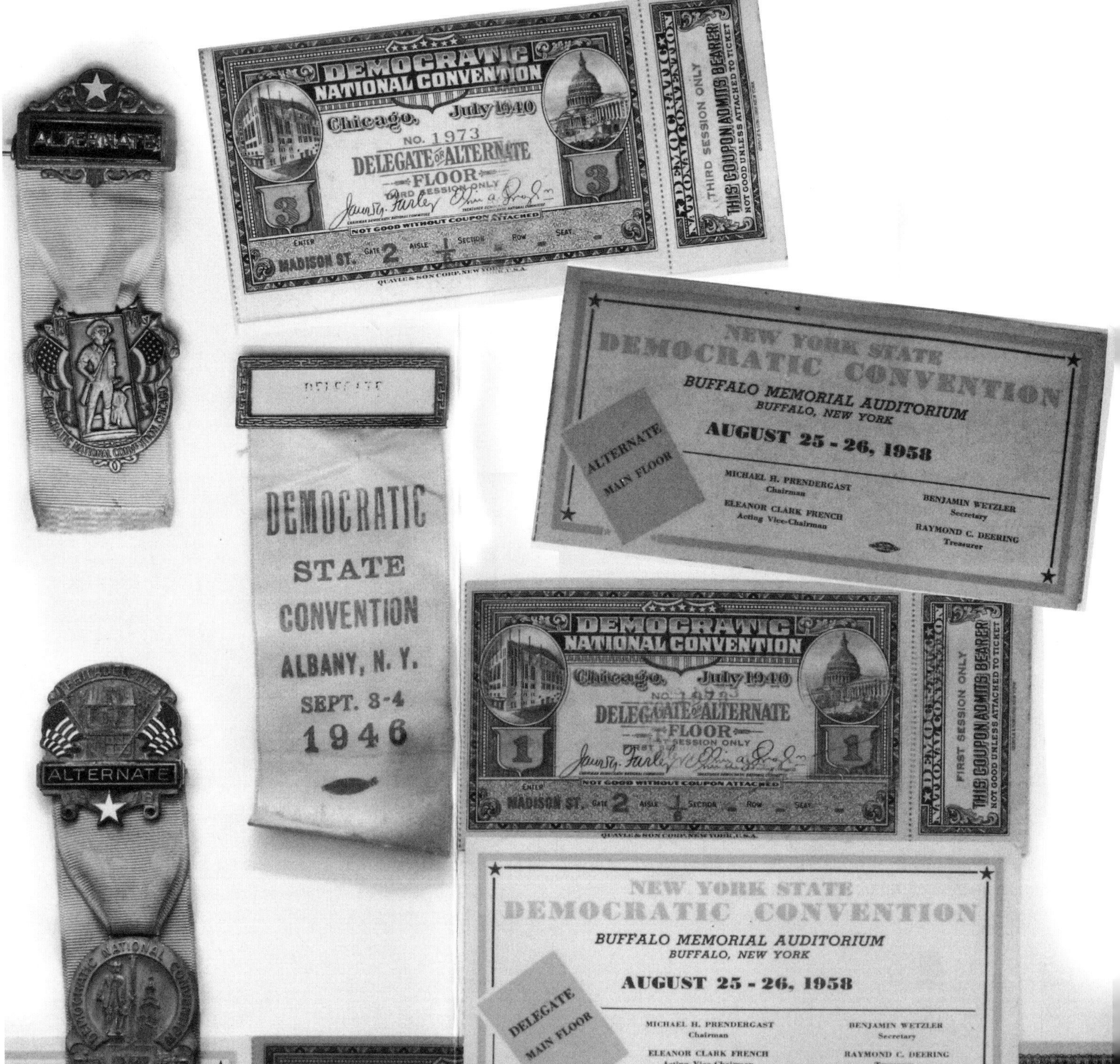

ALTERNATE
DEMOCRATIC NATIONAL CONVENTION
Chicago, July 1940
No. 1973
DELEGATE OR ALTERNATE
FLOOR
THIRD SESSION ONLY
NOT GOOD WITHOUT COUPON ATTACHED
MADISON ST. GATE 2
THIRD SESSION ONLY
THIS COUPON ADMITS BEARER
NOT GOOD UNLESS ATTACHED TO TICKET
NEW YORK STATE DEMOCRATIC CONVENTION
BUFFALO MEMORIAL AUDITORIUM
BUFFALO, NEW YORK
AUGUST 25 - 26, 1958
ALTERNATE MAIN FLOOR
MICHAEL H. PRENDERGAST Chairman
ELEANOR CLARK FRENCH Acting Vice-Chairman
BENJAMIN WETZLER Secretary
RAYMOND C. DEERING Treasurer
DELEGATE
DEMOCRATIC STATE CONVENTION ALBANY, N. Y. SEPT. 3-4 1946
DEMOCRATIC NATIONAL CONVENTION
Chicago, July 1940
DELEGATE OR ALTERNATE
FLOOR
FIRST SESSION ONLY
NOT GOOD WITHOUT COUPON ATTACHED
MADISON ST. GATE 2
FIRST SESSION ONLY
THIS COUPON ADMITS BEARER
ALTERNATE
DEMOCRATIC NATIONAL CONVENTION
NEW YORK STATE DEMOCRATIC CONVENTION
BUFFALO MEMORIAL AUDITORIUM
BUFFALO, NEW YORK
AUGUST 25 - 26, 1958
DELEGATE MAIN FLOOR
MICHAEL H. PRENDERGAST Chairman
ELEANOR CLARK FRENCH Acting Vice-Chairman
BENJAMIN WETZLER Secretary
RAYMOND C. DEERING Treasurer
DEMOCRATIC NATIONAL CONVENTION
Chicago, July 1940
SECOND BALCONY
NOT GOOD WITHOUT COUPON ATTACHED
THIS COUPON ADMITS BEARER
DEMOCRATIC CONV
ST GEORGE HOTEL
CONVENTION HALL
3RD SESSION ONLY
DELEGATE or ALTER
MAIN FLOOR
CHAIRMAN
SECRETARY
NOT GOOD WITHOUT COUPON AT

Introduction

by Phil Bean

Perched on a high hilltop in the mountainous interior of southern Italy, the village of Pignola, the ancestral home of Rufus P. Elefante, very briefly played a minor role in the battles that led to the Unification of Italy in 1860. Later in life, Elefante proudly boasted that members of his family in Pignola had participated in the armed rebellion led by Giuseppe Garibaldi that created modern Italy. Elefante also suggested that his relatives had then rebelled (as some people did) against the new government of united Italy when that government turned out not to be what they had anticipated. Elefante's life story was reflective of a belief, implicit in these tales, that power was an unavoidable reality, and that fighting for it was honorable, justifiable, and a measure of one's worth.

Although he was born into ethnic working-class obscurity and attained financial prosperity and the leadership of a long-successful, classic urban political organization—or "machine"—Elefante's life was hardly devoid of adversity; although he lived into his nineties, many of those close to him passed on before their time, and the political organization he led, and he himself, became, rightly or wrongly, the target of sometimes bitter criticism. Nevertheless, Elefante continued into his eighties, often with surprising success, his struggle to remain a significant player in the life of his community. Some objected to his persistence and to the longevity of his political career, and many others, particularly in the historically Italian neighborhood known as East Utica, defended him and heeded his advice into the closing decades of the twentieth century. Like him or not, one might in fairness concede (as have both scholars of national standing and even many of his local detractors) that Elefante's attainments were noteworthy for a man of his ethnic and socioeconomic background, education, time, and place.

Elefante's parents, Pasquale Elefante and Angela Maria (or Angelina) Paciello, were born and, in circa 1886-87, married in Pignola, a village located in the region of Basilicata (specifically Basilicata's province of Potenza), the most impoverished region in Italy. As happened in many southern Italian agricultural communities, Pignola's economic viability was undermined by overpopulation and economic change that pushed more and more of its inhabitants into poverty.

Even when work was to be had, living conditions were tenuous at best for much of Pignola's population. Peasants could hope for no more than 3-4 months of paid work per year, and their diet typically consisted largely of beans and potatoes; meat and pasta were rarities even after emigration had reduced the local labor supply and raised wages accordingly.

Even the relatively fortunate were hardly secure because it was difficult to prosper, particularly in a small agricultural community, when one's neighbors could not. Those who could emigrate therefore increasingly did so, typically in the hope of earning enough money in America to enable them to return home and buy the additional farmland that might stabilize their economic position. As a consequence, the population of Pignola spiraled downward from 4,000 in 1881 to 2,557 in 1901, and to 2,100 in 1907.

However, poverty does not in itself cause people to leave their homelands. The availability of increasingly cheaper transatlantic transportation in the late nineteenth century played a role in the outward mass migration of people from Pignola and towns like it, as did news that their townspeople, or *paesani*, had prospered as a result of their decision to emigrate at least temporarily to the United States. The mayor of Pignola reported in 1908 that, once this movement had begun, "emigrants who send money to their families" and those who, "returning from America after two or three years...build a little house or acquire an estate near the village," had encouraged, through their example, many other *pignolesi* to emigrate. The mayor also noted that letters from relatives and friends in America inspired many of his dwindling townspeople to emigrate.

Although Pasquale Elefante's family reportedly owned a small grove of fruit trees in Pignola which he had intended to cultivate for a living at the time of his marriage, there is no evidence that his family was particularly prosperous or that he could expect to earn more than a modest living if he had remained in Pignola. At the same time, his sister, Margaret Dolce, who had emigrated to the United States some years before, sent Pasquale letters encouraging him and his wife to join her in an American town named Utica.

Pasquale Elefante therefore followed his sister's advice and the example of other *pignolesi* who had already emigrated. He arrived, at the age of 24, in New York City aboard the *SS Neustria* on May 23, 1895, in the company of seven of his *paesani* from Pignola, five of whom were bound for Utica (misidentified in his ship manifest as "Ustica," the name of an island off the coast of Sicily); it is not clear when his wife Angela, who was not on the *Neustria*'s passenger list, joined Pasquale in Utica. Unlike some of their townspeople, Pasquale and Angela never returned to Italy. The couple eventually had seven children, all of them female except for Rufus Pasquale Elefante—widely known as "Rufie"—who was born in Utica on April 11, 1903. Rufie grew up in his family's modest two-story home, located at 309 First Street, within sight of Marino's Restaurant, the establishment that would serve as his future political headquarters.

Pasquale Elefante worked a number of jobs throughout his nearly 65 years living in Utica. First employed at Weaver's Brickyard, the elder Elefante also worked on the Barge Canal and the New York Central Railroad, as a custodian at Utica's Public Market, and eventually, in semi-retirement, as a watchman at his son's trucking business. His son Rufie attended Union Street School in Utica until he dropped out in the seventh grade. Leaving school at such a young age—when he was approximately 13 years old—was not uncommon among local Italians in that era.

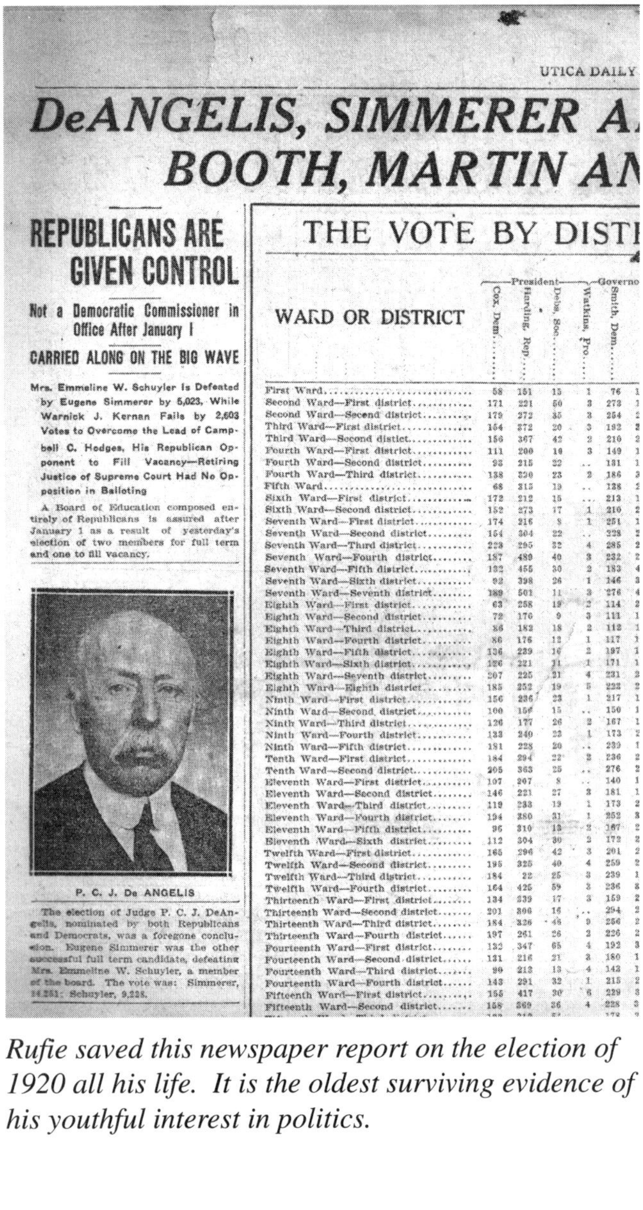

UTICA DAILY

DeANGELIS, SIMMERER A
BOOTH, MARTIN A

REPUBLICANS ARE GIVEN CONTROL

Not a Democratic Commissioner in Office After January 1

CARRIED ALONG ON THE BIG WAVE

Mrs. Emmeline W. Schuyler Is Defeated by Eugene Simmerer by 5,023, While Warnick J. Kernan Fails by 2,603 Votes to Overcome the Lead of Campbell C. Hodges, His Republican Opponent to Fill Vacancy—Retiring Justice of Supreme Court Had No Opposition in Balloting

A Board of Education composed entirely of Republicans is assured after January 1 as a result of yesterday's election of two members for full term and one to fill vacancy.

P. C. J. De ANGELIS

The election of Judge P. C. J. DeAngelis, nominated by both Republicans and Democrats, was a foregone conclusion. Eugene Simmerer was the other successful full term candidate, defeating Mrs. Emmeline W. Schuyler, a member of the board. The vote was: Simmerer, 14,251; Schuyler, 9,228.

THE VOTE BY DIST

WARD OR DISTRICT	President: Cox, Dem.	Harding, Rep.	Debs, Soc.	Watkins, Pro.	Governo: Smith, Dem.	
First Ward	58	151	15	1	76	1
Second Ward—First district	171	221	50	3	273	1
Second Ward—Second district	179	272	35	3	254	2
Third Ward—First district	164	372	20	3	192	2
Third Ward—Second distict	156	367	42	2	210	2
Fourth Ward—First district	111	200	16	3	149	1
Fourth Ward—Second district	93	215	22	..	131	1
Fourth Ward—Third district	138	230	23	2	186	3
Fifth Ward	68	313	13	..	138	2
Sixth Ward—First district	172	212	15	...	213	1
Sixth Ward—Second district	152	273	17	1	210	2
Seventh Ward—First district	174	216	8	1	251	1
Seventh Ward—Second district	164	304	22	..	228	2
Seventh Ward—Third district	223	295	32	4	285	2
Seventh Ward—Fourth district	187	489	40	3	232	2
Seventh Ward—Fifth district	132	455	30	2	183	4
Seventh Ward—Sixth district	92	398	26	1	146	3
Seventh Ward—Seventh district	189	501	11	3	276	4
Eighth Ward—First district	63	258	19	2	114	2
Eighth Ward—Second district	72	176	9	3	111	1
Eighth Ward—Third district	86	182	18	2	112	1
Eighth Ward—Fourth district	86	176	12	1	117	1
Eighth Ward—Fifth district	136	239	16	2	197	1
Eighth Ward—Sixth district	126	221	11	1	171	1
Eighth Ward—Seventh district	207	225	21	4	231	2
Eighth Ward—Eighth district	185	252	19	5	222	2
Ninth Ward—First district	156	236	23	1	217	1
Ninth Ward—Second district	100	156	15	..	150	1
Ninth Ward—Third district	126	177	26	2	167	1
Ninth Ward—Fourth district	133	240	22	1	173	2
Ninth Ward—Fifth district	181	228	20	..	239	1
Tenth Ward—First district	184	294	22	2	236	2
Tenth Ward—Second district	205	363	25	..	276	2
Eleventh Ward—First district	107	207	8	..	140	1
Eleventh Ward—Second district	146	221	27	3	181	1
Eleventh Ward—Third district	119	233	19	1	173	2
Eleventh Ward—Fourth district	194	280	31	1	252	3
Eleventh Ward—Fifth district	96	310	13	2	167	2
Eleventh Ward—Sixth district	112	304	30	2	172	2
Twelfth Ward—First district	165	296	42	3	201	2
Twelfth Ward—Second district	195	325	40	4	259	2
Twelfth Ward—Third district	184	22	25	3	239	1
Twelfth Ward—Fourth district	164	425	59	3	236	3
Thirteenth Ward—First district	134	339	17	3	159	2
Thirteenth Ward—Second district	201	306	16	..	294	2
Thirteenth Ward—Third district	184	326	48	9	256	2
Thirteenth Ward—Fourth district	197	261	26	2	226	2
Fourteenth Ward—First district	132	347	65	4	192	3
Fourteenth Ward—Second district	131	216	21	3	180	1
Fourteenth Ward—Third district	99	213	13	4	142	1
Fourteenth Ward—Fourth district	143	291	32	1	215	2
Fifteenth Ward—First district	155	417	30	6	229	3
Fifteenth Ward—Second district	158	369	26	4	228	3

Rufie saved this newspaper report on the election of 1920 all his life. It is the oldest surviving evidence of his youthful interest in politics.

At a time when Utica's population was approximately 60,000, of whom about ten percent were Italian immigrants (or, together with their American-born children, as much as a third of the population by 1915-20), only several hundred Uticans finished high school annually, and a mere handful of these more highly educated Uticans were of Italian parentage. The low wages most immigrants earned in the unskilled jobs for which they were qualified, and the drive to build up family economic resources, made the completion of primary school, let alone high school, a luxury few immigrant families were willing or able to allow their children, particularly their male children, in the early twentieth century.

Rufie Elefante therefore worked, as a young man, as baggage carter at Utica's railroad station, as a streetcar maintenance man for the Utica Transit Company, and as an apprentice in the Firsching Machine Shop, where he learned to repair the machinery used in local textile mills. However, it was through his endeavors in the field of politics, which began informally when he was still a schoolboy, that Rufie Elefante would find his avenue to success and distinction. Indeed, his encounters with anti-Italian

Rufie at the First Street house

prejudice at the Utica Transit Company and at Firsching's helped to drive Rufie to the conclusion that his ambitions, as a young Italian American with little education, might be attained only through active involvement in politics.

The Utica in which the Elefante family had settled was a community dominated by Protestants of "Yankee stock" (that is, of New England ancestry) whose forbears had settled Oneida County and by the newly-ascendant Irish American socioeconomic and political elite. The Yankee establishment also owned the textile mills in which much of thc immigrant population labored for low wages. Other groups, notably German and Welsh immigrants and their descendants, were locally numerous and counted among their number many successful businessmen, but from the perspective of the local power structure, they were of secondary importance, at best.

The Italians, Poles, eastern European Jews, and other southern and eastern Europeans who had begun to settle in Utica in noticeably increasing numbers since the 1880s and 1890s were therefore barely breaking into the lower ranks of the local socioeconomic and political "establishment" when Rufie was born. However, this is not to say that Italians were entirely without a voice in local political life. In 1900-10, Salvatore "Pop" Pellettieri (not "Bolottieri," as he has been inaccurately identified on occasion since the early 1990s), an immigrant from the village of Laurenzana in the province of Potenza and one of the first Italians to settle in Utica, and Vincenzo Marrone, an immigrant wholesaler from Potenza's village of Missanello, allied with James Schoolcraft Sherman, Utica's Republican Congressman and later Vice President of the United States. Italians, notably Antonio Sisti and Frank Brindisi (or "Brendes"), were important figures in local Italian Democratic life, but most Italians in Utica were Republican into the 1920s; indeed, Rufie began his career as an apprentice to local Republicans well before he was old enough to vote.

Although they were very much junior partners in their respective local political party organizations in the opening decades of the twentieth century, within the Italian *colonia*, the neighborhood known as East Utica, men like Salvatore Pellettieri drew to themselves talented and ambitious young men and boys who, recognizing they were not likely to prosper by laboring in Utica's mills, construction companies, and transportation companies, saw in politics an opportunity to enjoy social mobility, influence, and respect.

Pasquale and Angela Elefante's house on First Street, along side the Canal.

Indeed, neighborhood machine politicians would actively cultivate bright and energetic youngsters to serve as errand boys at election time. It was in this way that Elefante became a follower of "Pop" Pellettieri—the most influential local Italian prior to 1920—and Pellettieri's lieutenant, Alfred Bertolini. Already at the age of ten, Elefante had begun his political apprenticeship by handing out campaign literature for Republican candidates, and soon thereafter, he also began helping to round up Italian voters and bring them to the polls at the behest of his mentors. When Elefante was only 16 years old, Pellettieri hired him to serve as his personal driver.

That year, 1919, was a disruptive, formative moment in the history of the Italian community in Utica. Workers had tolerated steep inflation, and with the First World War over, East Utica's textile workers, hoping for better wages, went out on a long, bitter, and costly strike in which local police harassed, clubbed, arrested, and even shot and wounded Italian strikers. The strike politically mobilized Italians more than ever before, as Italian voters, angry at the city administration for its apparent favoritism toward mill owners, played a crucial role in toppling a previously popular mayor at the polls in 1919. As Elefante was heading toward adulthood, leadership of the local Italian community was therefore becoming much more prized than ever before, and it was also becoming clear to forward-thinking political leaders outside as well as inside the Italian community that the Italian vote was destined to become a pivotal, indeed, increasingly decisive factor in local politics.

On October 10, 1921, Salvatore "Pop" Pellettieri died, thus setting off an initially quiet power struggle from which Elefante eventually emerged as the political leader of East Utica and as a Democrat, not a Republican. Alfred Bertolini officially succeeded Pellettieri as the principal local Italian Republican leader, but his grasp on power was more precarious than it seemed. The year 1921 was generally bad for local Republicans, and the local press observed that Bertolini's position as Pellettieri's successor was crucially enhanced by the electoral success of his candidate for alderman of the First Ward, Frank Marino. However, in Marino's victory were the seeds of a dispute that would ultimately upend the political balance of power in East Utica and, eventually the city of Utica and even Oneida County.

Rufie in Havana, Cuba

Rufie's wife, the former Mary Zangrone, circa 1945.

The young Rufie Elefante had reportedly aspired to a political job that his Republican patrons had failed to give him. Those very same erstwhile patrons were now supporting another young Italian, Frank Marino, for alderman of Elefante's home ward. Although the fine details of the dispute are lost to time, it should not be surprising that Elefante saw in all of this the threat of growing political marginalization. He therefore began to contest Marino's position in the First Ward and generally to challenge the position of Marino's patron, Alfred Bertolini, as the principal political leader of Utica's Italian voters. Elefante abandoned the Republicans, and by 1923-24, before he was old enough to vote, he had pushed aside several more experienced non-Italian politicians to become the Democratic leader of the First Ward.

In 1925, Marino lost his bid for re-election to the city council. In the court battle that ensued, Marino contended he had lost only because Democrats from the nearby Fifth Ward had voted illegally in the First. Elefante was called to testify at the court hearing at which Marino contested the 1925 election results to respond to charges that Marino had been defeated due to voting irregularities. In his testimony, Elefante boldly scoffed at Marino's complaints and emerged unscathed. Although Marino convinced the court to overturn his defeat and served another term as the Republican alderman of the First Ward, Democrat and Elefante ally Daniel Laino defeated him in 1927. Elefante thus progressively extended his power across East Utica, and in fact Marino eventually changed parties, became a key Rufie loyalist, and was elected in 1931 as the Democratic alderman of the Fifth Ward. Although Bertolini managed to hold on politically until he died on the eve of the municipal elections of 1929, his position therefore had become increasingly shaky as a result of the growing influence of Elefante and the Democratic Party in East Utica.

Elefante was moving forward largely by virtue of hard work and his own natural talents, which made him astute in recognizing and making the best of opportunities. However, his alliance with two talented rising local Democratic leaders, Charles Donnelley (Mayor in 1929-33 and Postmaster of Utica in 1935-55) and Utica attorney M. William Bray (Chair of the New York State Democratic Committee in 1928-30 and Lieutenant Governor of New York in 1933-39) were crucial in facilitating his rise. Bray was a particularly important mentor to the young Elefante.

Elefante's position solidified further as a result of the candidacies of Alfred E. Smith and Franklin D. Roosevelt in the late 1920s and 1930s. Smith served as Governor of New York (1919-21 and 1923-28) and was the Democratic nominee for the presidency of the United States in 1928—indeed, the first Catholic to run for the presidency as the nominee of one of the two major parties. The failure of Smith's presidential run in 1928 stemmed to some extent from profound anti-Catholic, anti-Semitic, anti-urban, and generally anti-immigrant sentiment in much of the United States. The fact that Smith was demonized as the friend of people, like Italians, whom many Americans considered genetically inferior, hopelessly ignorant, unassimilable, and politically dangerous to America, helped to make Smith, and the Democratic Party that had dared to nominate him, all the more popular among Utica's Italian Americans.

In alliance with men of Bray and Donnelley's stature, Elefante got access to patronage, particularly after the victory of Franklin Roosevelt in the gubernatorial election of 1928. The future President entered the race late for Governor in 1928, and many doubted that, as a disabled person, he was equal, physically, to the challenges of office. Roosevelt therefore conducted an aggressive campaign tour throughout upstate New York to drum up support and to demonstrate his vigor. In Utica, Elefante and his allies organized for the visiting FDR a large and successful series of campaign events, including a rally attended by a reported 10,000 Uticans—largely Italian Americans—a parade down East Utica's main artery, Bleecker Street, and a capacity rally in a local theater that was broadcast by radio throughout central and western New York. This successful series of events in Utica and the margin of FDR's local success in East Utica boosted Elefante's standing in state party circles and paved the way to his becoming a leading figure in local politics for at least a half century.

Oneida County, and its largest city, Utica, was controlled throughout much of its history by less than a half dozen political "bosses," all of whom eventually came under severe criticism: Orsamus Matteson, the Republican son of early Yankee settlers, was widely acknowledged to be the first person to use money to influence local voters and was one of the few people ever driven from the House of Representatives under threat of expulsion when allegations arose in the late 1850s that he sought to corrupt fellow Congressmen; Roscoe Conkling, a Republican and, like Matteson, the son of settlers from New England, was the ruthless, arrogant boss of the state Republican machine and therefore controlled Oneida County political life in the 1870s and early 1880s; James S. Sherman, likewise a Republican of Yankee stock, and his Irish American allies, notably the unsavory Thomas Wheeler, dominated local politics, sometimes by use of somewhat questionable means, for much of the period between the mid-1880s and 1910; and Elefante and his allies were virtually the arbiters of political life in Utica and, increasingly, Oneida County, between the mid-1920s and the late 1950s.

Elefante was not the most publicly eminent of Utica's political kingmakers in the sense that, unlike Matteson, Conkling, Wheeler, and Sherman, he never occupied elective office, and he held appointive office only twice, and only briefly, in a career spanning six decades. However, Elefante was one of New York's most enduring machine politicians. Even after his influence began to decline, he played a sometimes deciding role in local politics into the 1980s, making him a leader or, if you will, "boss," whose longevity was rivaled in New York State only by Albany's Democratic titan, Dan O'Connell.

Recognized in the press—not just the local newspapers, but often by such national-circulation publications as the *New York Times*—for much of his life as a dominant force in what was once a politically key upstate county, Elefante's broader significance in the history of American urban politics was also acknowledged by scholars in the closing years of his life. By that point, both his detractors and supporters had correctly come to see in him one of the last of the white ethnic urban working-class politicians who had wrested power from older elites during the 1920s and 1930s only to be marginalized not just by critics but by changing times in the decades after World War II. His life story, in short, makes for good telling. In the memorabilia his family, principally his daughter, Angela, collected over the course of his career, we see a man of considerable tenacity and ingenuity. In pursuing such a long and active life, he had experiences that few people born into uneducated working-class immigrant families at the turn of the twentieth century could ever have considered likely, and he deeply affected the fortunes not just of his neighborhood, but of his home region.

Throughout the 1920s, as increasing numbers of Italians voted—and voted Democratic—Elefante had progressively consolidated his leadership position in East Utica. He reconciled with some important rivals, like Frank Marino, and built alliances with more established Italian Democrats like Rufus Cavallo. In addition, in many young Italian Democrats, most notably druggist Frank Emma, Rufie found loyal lieutenants and lesser allies who served the machine by registering new Democrats and getting out the vote in East Utica. The East Utica Smith for President Club, which Elefante had helped to lead, along with allies like Frank Emma, during the presidential election of 1928, was transformed after Smith's defeat into the "East Utica Democratic Club," which remained the main vehicle for the Elefante machine for decades thereafter.

After 1928, Elefante's importance rose because he and his allies had created a reliable Democratic voting bloc in a state that was more competitive for much of the twentieth century than its reputation as a training ground for such leading Democrats as Al Smith, Franklin D. Roosevelt, Mario Cuomo, and Daniel Patrick Moynihan might suggest. The Democratic Party's prospects for victory often hinged at least partly on its ability to get working-class white ethnics to vote for its candidates in the handful of more urbanized industrial counties in generally rural, white Protestant, heavily Republican upstate New York. And for those who successfully delivered Democratic votes, there were rewards. For instance, among the ways Governor Franklin Roosevelt showed his gratitude to his friends in Utica was reportedly to channel (quite legally) state hauling contracts through Elefante's trucking company which, among other things, helped Elefante accumulate financial resources that helped to fuel the East Utica Democratic political machine.

Elefante, as well as his allies both inside and outside East Utica, recognized the power of the press in helping to shape political opinion in East Utica. In the run-up to the 1932 presidential election, the East Utica Democratic organization therefore established its own weekly, *La Stella* ("The Star," the symbol of the Democratic Party), which continued in publication at least until the Utica municipal elections of 1933. Elefante's magazine excoriated Republicans and extolled the virtues of Franklin Roosevelt, other state and national Democratic Party leaders, the leaders of the local Democratic machine—including, to be sure, Elefante himself—and the gospel of the emerging New Deal. Perhaps even before the demise of *La Stella* in the fall of 1933, the cause of the Democratic Party in East Utica was also being championed journalistically by the principal local Italian-language newspaper, *Il Messaggiero dell'Ordine* ("The Messenger of Order"). Indeed, even after it switched to a largely English-language format in 1944 and became known as *The Messenger*, this publication continued to support Elefante's organization and the New Deal, and it periodically accused the Republican Party of being anti-Italian.

Italian Americans to a very large degree inhabited their own world, separate, to no small degree, from the rest of the local community, and for many years Elefante's rise therefore generally escaped the notice of the mainstream press. He seems first to have attained the notice of the local press as a result of Marino's successful attempt in court to overturn his defeat for re-election as the alderman of the First Ward in 1925. In the election of 1928, in which Al Smith, the New York Governor many Italians recognized as a friend of immigrants, became the Democratic nominee for the presidency, Elefante again emerged very briefly in the pages of the local newspapers as an official in the Smith for President campaign in East Utica. However, press coverage became both more frequent and less flattering in the early 1930s. In the elections of 1933, Elefante emerged for the first time on the pages of the national press in a brief report in the *New York Times* on charges that he had thrown Republican poll watchers bodily from a polling place in his center of power, the First Ward. The next year, he was likened, in essence, to the bogeyman, along with Bray and Donnelley, in an editorial cartoon in the Utica newspapers. To deaden the controversy over his growing prominence and the growing power of his Democratic machine, in 1934 Elefante dramatically made the first of a fairly long string of announcements that he was retiring from politics.

However, critics of the Elefante organization were generally ineffectual in this period because the machine delivered help that many people desperately needed, he had a firm control over the local Democratic organization, and the Republican Party was discredited in the eyes of so many Americans in the 1930s. In response to the hardship arising from the Depression,

Utica's Democratic city administration, which came to office soon after the stock market crash of 1929, increased local unemployment relief spending. In addition, the national Democratic New Deal brought public works projects to Utica, putting thousands, including many Italians, to work, and in the process, with all this construction, Rufie's trucking company picked up more contracts for hauling stone and other excavated material. By the end of the 1930s, even the *New York Times* acknowledged that the Italian vote, now predominantly Democratic, was crucial to determining elections not just in Utica but Oneida County. With Italian voters being so crucial to the fortunes of the Democratic Party in central New York, Elefante increasingly came into his own.

Elefante's success in business and politics began to win him the respectability and friends that a semi-educated ethnic working-class kid from East Utica could hardly have hoped to earn. He developed an apparently warm political friendship with Charles Poletti, one of the rising Italian American stars of New York State Democratic life. Even more widely famous figures as Joe Dimaggio broke bread with Rufie at his headquarters, Marino's Restaurant. In short, for so many, the 1930s was a time of tribulation, but the Depression cemented the position Elefante and his Democratic organization had earned through careful coalition-building in the 1920s, picking their friends well, supporting Al Smith's unsuccessful quest for the presidency in 1928, and advocating on behalf of activist government at a time in America's history in which many people now enthusiastically welcomed government help.

1930s

April - 20 - 1932

DEMOCRATS NAME EMMA, ELEFANTE

East Utica Club Elects Eighth Ward Alderman as President

RUFUS ELEFANTE THE LEADER

Officials Designated at Session for Reorganization

At the organization of the East Utica Democratic Club last night Frank A. Emma, alderman of the Eighth Ward, was named president. At a subsequent meeting of the committeemen and the ward leaders, Rufus Elefante was named East Utica leader for the Democrats.

Other officers of the East Utica Democratic Club: Corresponding secretary, Rufus Davoli; treasurer, Agnes Baker; directors, Rufus Cavallo, chairman, Joseph L. Matt, Joseph Elasmar, Jacob Ferletti, Daniel Laino, Frank A. Emma, Frank Marino, R. P. Cavallo, Supervisor Frank Ricco, Supervisor Thomas Ruggiero, Sam Curcio, Salvatore DeTraglia, Peter Andrello, Michael Collins; ward leaders, Eighth, Alderman Frank A. Emma; Fifth, Alderman Frank Marino; First, Alderman Daniel Laino.

All committeemen of the three wards were present at last night's meeting which was held in the Sisti Building, where club rooms have been established. The next meeting of the club will be April 25.

RUFUS ELEFANTE

Leader Democratico dell'East Utica, ha dato e da' tutte le sue giovani energie a pro del Partito e perche' i Democratici dell'East Utica, uniti tutti e sotto la sua abile guida, lavorino per il Partito e le idealita' di esso.

Instancabile nella sua attivita', fermo nei suoi propositi, egli guida le forze democratiche italiane nelle loro attivita' che assicureranno, a Novembre, la vittoria.

Siamo sicuri che i democratici dell'East Utica non si lasceranno ingannare dalle false manovre politiche degli avversari e daranno tutta la loro cooperazione al signor Elefante.

Don Dero
1118 Stark

VOL. II. UTICA, N. Y., SEPTEMBER 5, 1933 No. 18

LA STELLA

"THE STAR" - Italian-American Weekly

An Italo-American Newspaper with an American heart and an Italian soul.

Dedicated to American Citizenship ... the States ... America

S. DI DARIO, Editor and Publisher :-: :-: :-: :-: :-: S. CAPORALE, Managing Editor

RUFUS ELEFANTE
East Utica Democratic Leader

One of the youngest of our Italian leaders, and one who has risen to great heights in the community, is Rufus Elefanti, the recognized leader of the Democratic Party in East Utica. Although just past his thirtieth birthday, Rufie Elefanti has established for himself a place of power and influence rarely attained by men twice his age.

His parents were Pasquale Elefanti and Angelina Paciello and he first saw the light of day in Utica. Of a somewhat restless nature but always exceedingly industrious, by the time he had reached voting age he had attained a vast store of information on public matters and political matters. His pleasant manner, cheerful disposition, and his ever ready willingness to be of service to someone else, drew about him a host of loyal friends.

He had a natural flair for politics and although he never held public office, he has been responsible for an immense number of people being elected to office. There are few Italians of prominence who have not benefitted by his influence at one time or another in the past few years.

So outstanding had his influence become five years ago that he was the unanimous choice of his party for the important position of leader. It sometimes happens that a man is voted into a position of this kind but upon assuming the office finds that he has no great number to lead. In this case it was different for, as a matter of fact, Rufus Elefanti did not have to be proclaimed leader by vote of his fellows. He had already attained that position by common consent.

Mr. Elefanti married Mary Zangrone and he has one daughter, Angelina. He is head of R. Elefanti & Co., engaged in hauling and general contracting, and is a successful businessman as well as a successful politician. He is a member of the Knights of Columbus, Loyal Order of Moose, the Mohawk Athletic Club, the Democratic Club and many other organizations, and attends St. Mary of Mount Carmel Church.

The things that endear Rufus Elefanti to his large circle of friends are his frank, open nature, his great generosity, and his constant desire to help others. It is said of him that he never went back on a friend or disregarded in the slightest degree a promise or an obligation which he had assumed. His friends confidently predict for him even greater honors than have already come to him.

left to right: Joe Marino, Rufus Cavallo, Danny Laino, Frank Marino, Jim Ricco, Rufie, unidentified gentleman, Frank Emma

Tom and Theresa Ruggiero, Isabel Laino, Rufie

DO YOU WANT SLOAN OR ELEFANTE?

The Voters of The City of Utica Are Urged To:

1—KEEP OUT THE DEMOCRATIC CANDIDATE, CORROU, THE NOMINEE AND FIGUREHEAD OF ELEFANTE, BRAY AND DONNELLEY. TWO YEARS AGO, THE CITY TURNED THESE THREE OUT. DO YOU WANT THEM BACK AGAIN?

Elefante, speaking at a Democratic Rally for Corrou, said, "This is not a fight between Corrou and Sloan, this is my fight."

CORROU'S HALLOWE'EN PARADE

HE CAN'T COVER THEM UP . . .

So He Won't Talk!

RUFUS ELEFANTE

Elefante Is Silent On Reports About His Political Speech

Rufus (Rufie) Elefante, East Utica Democratic leader, declined to comment today on published reports that he made an important political speech in the campaign this week.

He was quoted by Earle C. Bastow, first assistant district attorney, as saying that the municipal election was a test to find out if he should be returned to power in Utica.

When seen this morning Rufie told an O-D reporter he "didn't know how to make a speech," but wanted to confer with Charles A. McKernan before giving out any statement at all.

At noon he issued a typewritten statement reading: "Any statement that is made by me now would be distorted as my statements in the past have been distorted. I have nothing further to say."

Elefante said he is now in the contracting business in partnership with Ald. Daniel Laino of the First Ward and the two of them own 18 large trucks to carry on their business.

Buone Feste a Tutti

Frank A. Emma

Rufus P. Cavallo

Rufus Elefante

You are cordially invited to attend the Inauguration
of
Herbert H. Lehman
as Governor of the State of New York
in the Assembly Chamber of the State Capitol at Albany
January first, nineteen hundred and thirty-seven
at twelve o'clock noon

Joe Marino, unidentified, "Sharkey," Johnny Belmont, Mike Tofolo, unidentified, unidentified, behind Rufie, Tom Ruggiero, Rufie, to the left unidentified, Jim Kipper with hat and two unidentified gentleman

Dinner at Frank Sisti's house. Agnes and Anna Sisti, Frank Sisti, Rufie, and Tony Sisti, City Clerk

Marino's Restaurant – Dino Pucine, waiter

Identifiable: Rufie Cavallo, Sam Vatalaro, Mike Tofolo, Fay Bennett, Marty Kozlowski, "Mushkey" (Joe Romano), Joe Fiore, Dorothy DiMaggio, Joe DiMaggio, Rufie

Vol. XVII. Utica, N. Y., October 30, 1937 Num. 40

IL MESSAGGIERO

DELL'ORDINE

Phone 2-0512 Phone 2-0512

formerly L'ORDINE

The Oldest Italian Weekly of Oneida County P. Amitrano, Owner—966 Bleecker St.

Entered as second class matter April 2, 1921, at the Post Office at Utica, New York, under the Act of March 3, 1879

Republicans are against the Italians & E. Utica!

Why do the Republicans always attack the Italians before each election? Why does the Republican Party throw mud on the character and good citizenship of Utica's Italian citizens just before each election?

Two years ago, just before election, you remember the indecent attack upon Utica's Italian citizens in paid advertisements. The Italian-Americans RESENTED this undeserved DISCRIMINATION against them by the Republican mud-throwers. The Italian citizens of Utica voted AGAINST such UN-AMERICAN DISCRIMINATION and CORROU became Mayor.

309 First st.

CHARLES POLETTI
DELEGATE AT LARGE

STATE OF NEW YORK
THE CONSTITUTIONAL CONVENTION
ALBANY

July 18, 1938.

Rufus Elefante, Esq.,
Utica,
New York.

Dear Rufus:

Many times I have thought of the wonderful time I had in your home. You and Mrs. Elefante were exceedingly gracious and I enjoyed every moment I was there, especially that fine pizza.

With warm regards,

Yours sincerely,

Charles Poletti

Tony De Gironemo,
President Common Council,
City Clerk

Salvador Capecelatro,
"Chickala,"
Fred Tomaino,
two unidentified,
Rufie,
Senatro Paladino,
Rufie Cavallo

Freddy Tomaino,
Rufie,
Rufie Cavallo,
Carl DelBuono,
Nick Rizzo

The 1940s

At the onset of the 1940s, Elefante was approaching the apex of his influence. Locally, as Bill Bray began slowly to fade in importance, Elefante began his long relationship with Richard Balch, a young manufacturer who would become the unsuccessful Democratic nominee for Lieutenant Governor in 1950, Chair of the State Democratic Committee, and manager of the (unsuccessful) presidential campaign of Averell Harriman, who became Governor of New York in 1954. Like Elefante—and unlike Bray—Balch was allied with the ascendant pro-New Deal faction of the state party led by Bronx Democratic boss and later Democratic national committeeman Edward J. Flynn. In addition to allying more closely with Flynn against party conservatives, Elefante evidently continued for at least some years to maintain his close political acquaintance with Charles Poletti, who became Lieutenant Governor of New York in 1938 and served very briefly as New York's first Italian American Governor in 1942.

Elefante also developed a politically profitable relationship with United States Senator James Mead of Buffalo, the unsuccessful Democratic nominee for Governor in 1946. Mead helped Utica's Democratic administration to secure federally-guaranteed loans to purchase the privately-owned Utica Water Company, which became an important, locally-regulated public utility (and source of patronage), in the late 1930s and helped to ensure that the wartime military installation later known as Griffiss Airforce Base, which eventually created thousands of local jobs, would remain in Oneida County.

In 1940, Elefante attended the first of four Democratic National Conventions (the others being 1944, 1948, and 1960). At the Democratic Convention of 1944, Rufie, ever the FDR loyalist, voted against the renomination of Henry Wallace (whom Roosevelt wanted to be dumped from the ticket) in favor of Harry Truman for the vice presidency. Elefante's increasingly close ties to New Deal loyalists and his own growing influence in upstate Democratic politics led to his being one of the relatively few people invited to gather on the south lawn of the White House to witness the brief, final inauguration of Franklin Roosevelt in January 1945.

While his political standing locally and within state Democratic circles was growing, Elefante's business likewise prospered. The trucking company he and his brother-in-law Peter Mazza had operated since the 1920s had expanded to the point at which, by the late 1940s, they owned a dozen and a half 18-ton trucks, which positioned them well to be a dominant force in the local construction hauling business. One of their largest contracts entailed the transportation of a million tons of crushed stone for the construction of the runways at the air force base in Rome in 1941-42.

The East Utica machine was riding high, but it faced a potential problem: Governor Thomas E. Dewey and the Republican-controlled state legislature. The Dewey administration took an aggressive stance toward cities statewide—chiefly New York City, Albany, and Utica—that were considered Democratic strongholds. Speaking through East Utica's newspaper, *The Messenger*, Elefante's machine accepted Dewey's challenge, accusing the Governor during his 1946 re-election bid of being a hypocrite and an enemy of organized labor and of veterans of the recent war; its most incendiary charge was that Dewey had authorized the State Police to use "Gestapo Methods" against opponents of the state administration. Such invective on the part of an East Utica machine that was approaching the height of its power undoubtedly antagonized local Republicans and may have played a role in Dewey's decision to pursue charges of corruption against Democratic leaders in Utica, as he had in New York City and Albany.

In 1949, with the active encouragement of Republicans in the legislature, Dewey secured the appointment of a special prosecutor who convened a special grand jury that eventually indicted Elefante and nine other local officials and Democratic political organizers, including two of Elefante's African American allies and his West Utica lieutenant, Denny O'Dowd. The prosecution, which consumed the second half of 1949, centered on charges that the defendants had violated state election laws in 1948 by, among other things, allegedly paying individual voters to cast their ballots for Democratic candidates. Mayor Golder came to the defense of Elefante and his codefendants, dismissing the investigation as part of a "preconceived plan to destroy the Democratic Party in Utica and Oneida County," and an "act of revenge" for the fact that Truman had won Oneida County in his upset victory over Governor Dewey in the presidential election of 1948.

Elefante and his codefendants were acquitted of all charges, and the organization continued on its upward march for another decade. In fact, disgust over the investigation, which many considered to have been politically-motivated and anti-Italian, may have intensified voter loyalty to Elefante in East Utica in the run-up to the 1950 elections. Nevertheless, in January 1950, the recently-acquitted Elefante announced yet again that he intended to step down as East Utica Democratic leader. As occurred with all other such announcements—and there were many—his 1950 leadership resignation did not have any meaningful impact on the reality that Elefante was the undisputed leader of an increasingly powerful local political organization.

1940s

Rufus P. Elefante e' sempre il riconosciuto ed apprezzato Leader dell'East Utica

Rufus P. Elefante

Il leader democratico dell'East Utica, Rufus P. Elefante, sentitamente ringrazia quanti sono stati con lui nelle elezioni ed hanno cosi' apprezzato quanto egli ha fatto per il benessere dell'East Utica e dei suoi cittadini.

Egli e' sempre al suo posto fiducioso e sereno e le innumerevoli prove di simpatie avute dimostrano che gode quella fiducia, che sara' messa a servizio dell'East Utica, specie se in un prossimo domani sara' necessaria una piu' sentita unione per meglio e piu' efficacemente tutelare i comuni interessi.

Rufus P. Elefante, Will Always Lead East Utica

The Leader of East Utica, Rufus P. Elefante, wishes to thank all who have cooperated with him during the past Election and have so proven their appreciation for all he has done towards the welfare of East Utica and all its citizens.

He has been and will always be our Leader and the innumerable proofs of admiration received this Election show only more plainly that he is still the pride and power of the citizens of East Utica and that he will always be ready, willing and able to offer a helping hand to all who may approach him in the future as in the past.

Democratic Convention Nominees

M. WILLIAM BRAY

DR. BRIAN J. KELLY

RUFUS ELEFANTE

RICHARD H. BALCH

BRAY, KELLY, BALCH, ELEFANTE FOR CONVENTION

Approximately 75 members of the Democratic city committee met last night and were given petitions for delegates and alternates to the Democratic national convention in Chicago from the 33rd Congressional District, comprising Oneida and Herkimer Counties.

The petitions are for Dr. Brian J. Kelly, Frankfort, and M. William Bray, Utica, for delegates and Rufus Elefante and Richard H. Balch, Utica, as alternates. This slate has been selected by the Democratic executive committees of the two counties and will be voted upon in the April primaries. No opposition has been indicated.

Bray Noncommittal

Dr. Kelly is known as a staunch organization—meaning Roosevelt—supporter, while Bray is noncommittal. His name has been reportedly allied with the Garner campaign, although he has denied it.

Balch and Elefante are generally considered to be Roosevelt supporters. Balch has served actively in the local Democratic organization and is chairman of the Municipal Water Commission, operating the supply and distribution system as a water bureau.

Elefante has been prominent in politics in this city for many years. Originally a Republican in his youth, he was elected East Utica Democratic leader several years ago by committeemen representing wards in that section of the city.

Petitions also were distributed to the various committeemen last night for their own candidates for re-election as city committeemen.

Brennan Presides

Stephen W. Brennan, former county chairman, presided at the meeting. He said he had been requested to prepare the petitions by Charles A. McKernan, county chairman, who has been confined in St. Elizabeth Hospital since Jan. 1.

Rep. Fred J. Douglas and Donald Brush, Herkimer County Republican leader, are the GOP national convention delegates from this district.

Victory Dinner Delayed By Heavy Bond Sale

LEADERS IN THE ITALIAN-AMERICAN DIVISION of the Second War Loan Drive who reported at least $106,000 subscribed last night toward the county's $8,681,000 are, left to right, Rufus Elefante, Rufus P. Cavallo and Santo Ferraro, talking with Charles W. Hall, right, an executive of the campaign.

Guests of the Italian-American Division of the Second War Loan Drive delayed the serving of a victory dinner for two hours last night in the Martin while subscriptions totaling at least $106,000 kept a volunteer War Bond sales force working at top speed at a special table near the entrance to the ballroom.

Francis P. McGinty, chairman of the county War Finance Committee, estimated the evening's sales had raised the total for the county, to date, to $8,681,000, and helped the county exceed its quota by $2,500,000.

Mayor Corrou, smilingly casting his vote in his home district in the 17th Ward yesterday.

The Vote in Utica

Repubiican	Democrat
MAYOR	
J. Maynard Jones, 14,999	Vincent Corrou, 24,41
COUNCIL PRESIDENT	
Fred Rogers, 13,983	Henry A. Smith, 23,03
CITY CONTROLLER	
I. E. Crade, 12,764	Thomas J. Nelson, 25,61
CITY TREASURER	
Irving Thurston, 11,335	Donald G. Price, 27,40
ASSOCIATE CITY JUDGE	
Smith Johnson, 13,281	Martin J. Lutz, 24,89
JUSTICE OF THE PEACE	
Henry J. Ziemba, 14,626	Walter M. Dowling, 23,84
ASSESSORS	
James C. Campbell, 13,536	Boyd E. Golder, 23,61
Charles F. Knapp, 10,464	Edward V. Donohue, 23,01
COUNTY TREASURER	
Gardner O. Hart, 14,526	George C. Moore, 22,28
CORONER	
Preston R. Clark, 16,391	Pasquale Montesano, 20,57

Unidentified, Rufie, Marty Kozlowski, Jim Kipper, Hottie Romanelli, two unidentified, Sam Vatalaro

Rufus Elefante Is Feted by Uticans

EAST UTICAN HONORED. Rufus Elefante is guest at a surprise party given by the Mohawk Athletics. A feature of the party was the music of four prominent Uticans. Left to right, Rufus P. Cavallo, deputy commissioner of public safety; Dr. James G. Douglas, Mr. Elefante and former Mayor Fred Rath.

Judge Walsh, Bridegroom-elect, Honored

CITY JUDGE FETED. Members of the Chauffeurs and Teamsters Union give dinner for John J. Walsh, who will be married Oct. 3 at Hudson. Left to right, Assemblyman Frank Emma, Postmaster Charles Donnelley, Rufus Elefante, Judge Walsh, Sheriff Bradbury J. German, Michael Wilsey, dinner chairman, and District Attorney Earle C. Bastow.

CA, N. Y., FRIDAY MORNING, OCTOBER 23, 1942

State Democratic Chairman James Bennett, Rufie, and Lieutenant Governor Charles Poletti.

NA56 16 SC=NEWYORK NY
RUFUS ELEFANTE=
UTICA NY=

MANY THANKS FOR ALL YOUR GOOD WORK KEEP UP THE FIGHT FOR DEMOCRATIC VICTORY WARM REGARDS=
CHARLIE POT POLETTI.

The honor of your presence
is requested at the ceremonies
attending the Inauguration of the
President of the United States
January twentieth,
Nineteen hundred forty-five.

Harry Flood Byrd, Chairman,
Kenneth McKellar, Arthur Vandenberg, Sam Rayburn,
Robert L. Doughton, Joseph W. Martin, Jr.
Committee on Arrangements.
Edwin A. Halsey, Secretary.

Please present the enclosed
card of admission.

Mr. Rufus P. Elefante

HONORED GUEST

Inauguration Ceremonies

JANUARY TWENTIETH, 1945

11:45 A. M.

ADMIT BEARER TO SECTION **B** OF THE WHITE HOUSE GROUNDS, LOCATED SOUTH OF THE PORTICO. ENTER EITHER SOUTHEAST OR SOUTHWEST GATE.

Harry F. Byrd
Chairman
Committee on Arrangements

NONTRANSFERABLE

Elefante Accuses Golder Foes Of Raising False Racial Issue

AT GOLDER DINNER—Checking over program with Boyd E. Golder, second from left, the guest of honor, are Rufus P. Cavallo, left, and Rufus P. Elefante, dinner committee heads, and Assemblyman Frank A. Emma, right, toastmaster.

Rufus P. Elefante, East Utica Democratic leader, charged last night that those opposing the candidacy of Boyd E. Golder for mayor are circulating the story that he is Jewish.

• • •

"If Boyd Golder should have been of Jewish extraction, we would have been just as proud to support him as we were to support Governor Lehman with our huge pluralities, and who was the best governor we ever had."

ELEFANTE said such tactics are nothing new. "It has been done time after time," he declared. "Ten years ago they were telling that Corrou (Vincent R. Corrou, former mayor and now state senator) was of Italian extraction."

"I am the leader of a section of the city where democracy is practiced. It is made up of Italian, Polish, Syrian, Irish and other races. We live together as neighbors and as friends."

Hold Conference On Relief For Italy

Left to right; U. S. Senator James M. Mead, Rufus P. Elefante, East Utica's Democratic leader and Senator Lister Hill, majority whip of U. S. Senate, emerging from a conference on Italian relief for Italy.

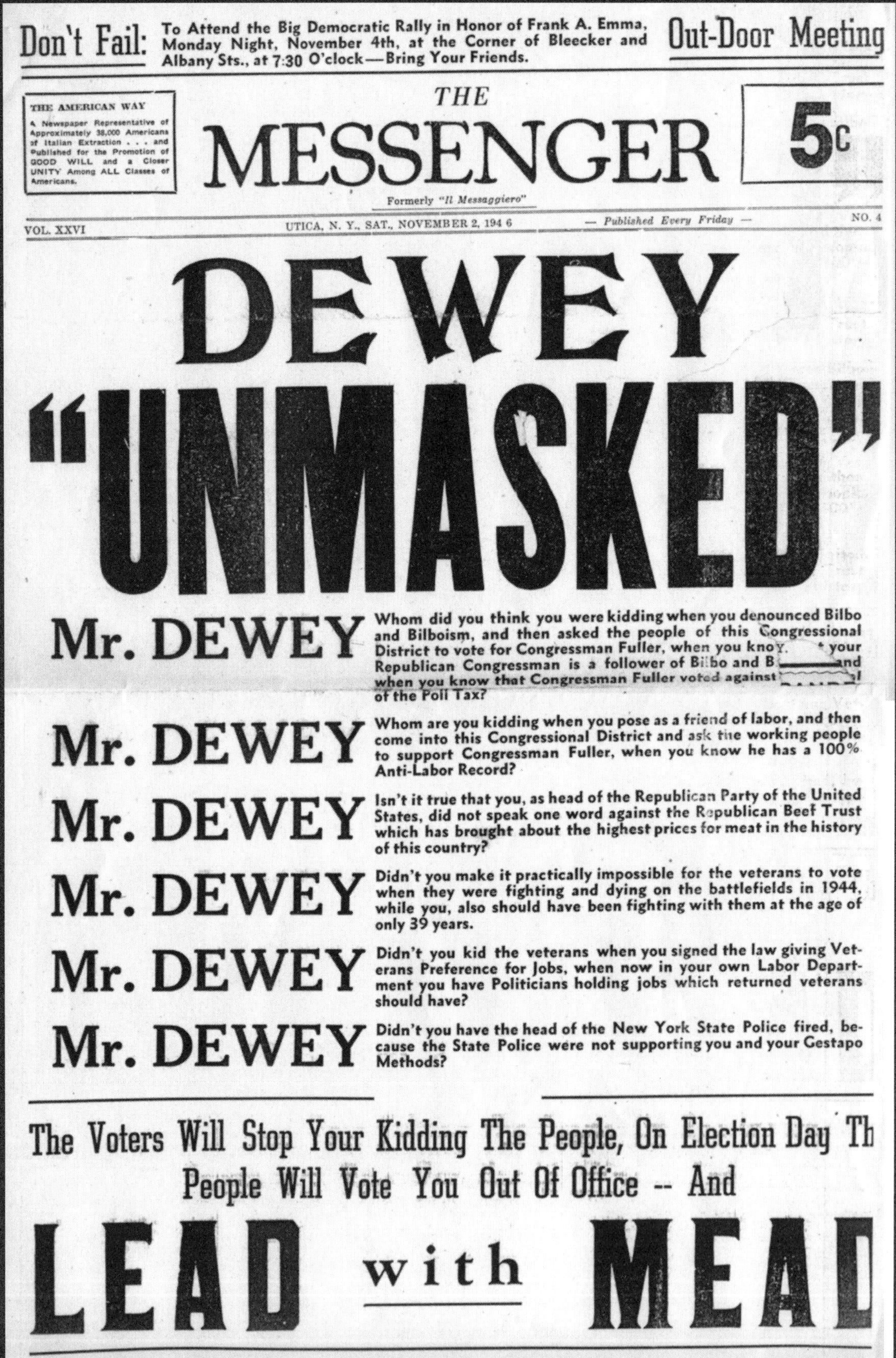

Don't Fail: To Attend the Big Democratic Rally in Honor of Frank A. Emma, Monday Night, November 4th, at the Corner of Bleecker and Albany Sts., at 7:30 O'clock—Bring Your Friends. **Out-Door Meeting**

THE AMERICAN WAY
A Newspaper Representative of Approximately 38,000 Americans of Italian Extraction . . . and Published for the Promotion of GOOD WILL and a Closer UNITY Among ALL Classes of Americans.

THE
MESSENGER
Formerly *"Il Messaggiero"*

5c

VOL. XXVI — UTICA, N. Y., SAT., NOVEMBER 2, 1946 — *Published Every Friday* — NO. 4

DEWEY
"UNMASKED"

Mr. DEWEY Whom did you think you were kidding when you denounced Bilbo and Bilboism, and then asked the people of this Congressional District to vote for Congressman Fuller, when you know [illegible] your Republican Congressman is a follower of Bilbo and B[illegible] and when you know that Congressman Fuller voted against [illegible] of the Poll Tax?

Mr. DEWEY Whom are you kidding when you pose as a friend of labor, and then come into this Congressional District and ask the working people to support Congressman Fuller, when you know he has a 100% Anti-Labor Record?

Mr. DEWEY Isn't it true that you, as head of the Republican Party of the United States, did not speak one word against the Republican Beef Trust which has brought about the highest prices for meat in the history of this country?

Mr. DEWEY Didn't you make it practically impossible for the veterans to vote when they were fighting and dying on the battlefields in 1944, while you, also should have been fighting with them at the age of only 39 years.

Mr. DEWEY Didn't you kid the veterans when you signed the law giving Veterans Preference for Jobs, when now in your own Labor Department you have Politicians holding jobs which returned veterans should have?

Mr. DEWEY Didn't you have the head of the New York State Police fired, because the State Police were not supporting you and your Gestapo Methods?

The Voters Will Stop Your Kidding The People, On Election Day Th People Will Vote You Out Of Office -- And

LEAD with MEAD

During the election of 1946, Rufie and his local allies launched an aggressive attack on the incumbent Republican governor, Thomas E. Dewey.

Rufus Elefante, East Utica Democratic Leader, Chosen Alternate

ELEFANTE ONLY ALTERNATE ELECTED FROM THIS AREA TO NATIONAL DEMOCRATIC CONVENTION

Rufus Elefante

Recently at a state committee meeting in New York City, Rufus Elefante, Democratic leader of East Utica, was elected as alternate to delegate-at-large to the Democratic National Convention. Twenty delegates-atlarge and twenty alternates were selected by the committee of which Mr. Elefante was the only one from this area.

Former Mayor Vincent R. Corrou and Richard H. Balch elected in the spring primary, are the regular delegates from this Congressional district.

Rufie and his allies
at the 1948 Democratic National Convention

UTICANS AT CONVENTION—Shown at the Democratic National Convention yesterday in Philadelphia are these four Utica men. From the left are Richard Balch, delegate; Rufus Elefante, East Utica leader; M. William Bray, a delegate and former lieutenant-governor of New York State, and Rufus P. Cavallo, Utica's deputy commissioner of public safety. (Acme Telephoto).

Vincent "Criggy" Fiore, Senatro Paladino, Rufie

Father Pizzoglio Gets $1,000 Check

Happy over a check for $1,000, presented him last night by the special gifts committee of St. Mary of Mount Carmel Church is the Rev. William Pizzoglio, pastor of the church, who is scheduled to leave about May 15 to visit his mother in Brazil. From the left are Rufus P. Cavallo, Father Pizzoglio, Anthony V. Sisti Jr., and Rufus P. Elefante. The presentation was made by Toastmaster Frank A. Emma and talks were given by Mayor Golder, Salvador J. Capecelatro and Joseph Cardamone. Father Pizzoglio is expected back Oct. 1.

Avanti, Sempre Avanti' East Utica

Con animo profondamente grato, o amici dell'East Utica, vi esprimo la mia ammirazione per la vostra fede e la vostra disciplina, che determinarono la grande vittoria elettorale di Martedi' scorso.

Ancora una volta avete dimostrato di saper difendere gl'ideali della democrazia — che e' guida luminosa per gli uomini liberi — e ancora una

RUFUS P. ELEFANTE

volta, malgrado circostanze avverse, mi avete riconfermato la vostra fiducia, che per me costituisce un sacro impegno per difendere i vostri diritti, onde raggiungere la meta delle vostre agognate aspirazioni.

Voi avete combattuto una grande battaglia ed avete dato al Partito Democratico la possibilita' di conseguire la piu' clamorosa vittoria, che, poi, e' la vostra vittoria.

Avanti, o amici dell'East Utica, sempre avanti.

Voi, d'altra parte, conoscete quanto in 25 anni io abbia saputo e potuto fare e sapete pure che avete acquistato una posizione politica, che e' e deve essere mantenuta e rispettata.

Ma tutto cio' che ho fatto, o amici dell'East Utica, e' esclusivamente merito vostro. Io ho potuto agire, perche' sono stato confortato dalla vostra costante fiducia, ed io ho potuto e posso parlare, perche' so che l'intera comunita' Italo-Americana e' pronta a far valere con il diritto del voto le sue buone ragioni.

Se guardate il passato avete la prova che molta strada si e' fatta, ed oggi l'East Utica e' una forza nobile ed attiva, che nella vita politica porta il piu' alto contributo di patriottismo e di capacita' perche' ha uomini che la sanno rappresentare.

La vostra salda unione, riconfermatasi Martedi' scorso, e' una garanzia per le lotte e le conquiste del domani.

Voi potete contare sulla mia devozione per gl'ideali e le mete che desiderate conseguire; io, poi, sono certo che tra voi e me sempre piu' si rafforzeranno i legami della comprensione e della mutua simpatia e, sorretto dalla vostra fiducia, io sento di avere tutta l'autorita' per potervi degnamente e proficuamente rappresentare.

Avete riconfermato alla nostra Citta' un'amministrazione organica e veramente progressiva. Il vostro merito e' grande. Ma non vi fermate a questa vittoria. L'anno prossimo la Nazione sara' chiamata a segnare i suoi destini, minacciati dalle correnti reazionarie.

Io, come sempre, saro' con voi ed in prima linea e voi dovrete concorrere a dare alla nostra Nazione un Governo, che salvaguardi i diritti della classe lavoratrice e promuova per il mondo quel benessere e quella pace, che sono le doloranti aspirazioni di tutti i popoli.

Ed, infine, mi e' assai gradito esternare il mio incondizionato plauso a quanti, uomini e donne dell'organizzazione Democratica dell'East Utica, hanno brillantemente compiuto il loro dovere, lavorando indefessamente per conseguire la vittoria dello scorso Martedi'.

Avanti, sempre avanti, o amici dell'East Utica.

RUFUS P. ELEFANTE,
East Utica Democratic
Leader.

Behind the Scenes At Vote Probe Trial

TRIAL STRATEGY is outlined by Maurice Supiro, counsel, to Rufus P. Elefante, East Utica Democrat, one of the 10 defendants in the vote probe trial yesterday.

1949

Mayor Calls Probe 'Sinister Scheme'

Mayor Golder yesterday branded the special grand jury investigation that has resulted in the indictment of Rufus P. Elefante, Dennis O'Dowd and others on conspiracy charges as a part of a sinister, revengeful scheme to destroy the Democratic Party in Utica and Oneida County.

He made the charge in a letter to enrolled Democrats urging them to register "and then vote the Democratic ticket in the true American spirit of crushing those who would use the power of public office to destroy our party."

Golder accused Governor Dewey to becoming a party to the scheme by ordering the special grand jury investigation. He said that in appointing a local attorney (Frank Pratt) who had lost his job through last year's election, as special prosecutor, the Governor had defeated the will of the people.

• • •

THE MAYOR SAID he was addressing the letter to voters of his party not only in behalf of his own election, but also "for the benefit of our Democratic Party and all the fine things it stands for.

"The present political campaign," he said, "is based on a preconceived plan to destroy the Democratic Party in Utica and Oneida County."

This is how he claims the plan developed:

"When President Harry S. Truman carried Oneida County and the Democrats elected a district attorney and a county clerk for the first time in many years, a certain clique became fearful that the Democrats would take control of Oneida County. Instead of accepting defeat in the normal American way, the spirit of revenge prevailed.

• • •

"THEY MADE an appeal to the Governor. He, too, being a defeated candidate in the City of Utica, became a party to the scheme by ordering a special grand jury, which is predominantly Republican and mostly non-residents of the city.

"Ignoring the choice of the people who had selected their own prosecuting attorney, the Governor appointed a special prosecutor, a local attorney who had lost his job through the election, and thereby defeated the will of the people.

"The final cost of this maneuver will be a shock to the local taxpayers' pocketbook. All of this investigation is at your expense and in a spirit of revenge. Is this the price that we have to pay in New York State for free elections?"

• • •

"THE FUTURE of our party is at stake," said Golder. "We can defeat this sinister scheme if every Democrat will register and then vote the Democratic ticket in the true American spirit of crushing those who would use the power of public office to destroy our party.

"Your last chance to register so that you can vote is this Friday, Oct. 14, and Saturday, Oct. 15."

Utica Observer-Dispatch

SECTION TWO | UTICA, N. Y., TUESDAY EVENING, DECEMBER 20, 1949 | PAGE ONE-A

Tears, Laughter Greet the Verdict; Trial Tension, Heartaches Forgotten

OL. LXVIII, NO. 241 | 18 PAGES | UTICA, N. Y., TUESDAY MORNING, DECEMBER 20, 1949 | ★ ★ ★ | PRICE FIVE CEN

NOT GUILTY ON ALL CHARGES, the seven vote probe trial defendants pose with their lawyers shortly after the jury brought in its verdict at 10:37 p. m. From the left, Ferdinand Tonmino, defense lawyer; Lawrence DePerno, Dennis P. O'Dowd, Lt. Martin J. Kozlowski, Jacob Goldbas, defense lawyer; Alderman Thomas J. Ruggiero, Paul Shanahan, chief defense counsel; Rufus P. Elefante, A. Fay Bennett, Maurice Supiro, defense lawyer and Elliott (Smiles) Johnson. (Photo by Dante Tranquille.)

The 1950s

In the very same year, 1949, in which the Dewey administration unsuccessfully prosecuted charges against Elefante, *Fortune* magazine held Utica up as a praiseworthy example of rational partnership between business and local government in the service of much-needed local economic transformation. As *Fortune* noted, Richard Balch, at that point only a year away from becoming the Democratic nominee for Lieutenant Governor of New York, was serving as an intermediary between the "boys at Marino's"—Elefante and his allies—and businessmen interested in promoting development ventures. If the East Utica machine did not initiate the local economic renaissance known as the "Loom to Boom" era, it played an important role in facilitating local economic renewal in the aftermath of the departure of textile manufacturing from Utica. Nevertheless, some did not appreciate the fact that the continuing success of these efforts depended on local political stability, as investors are less likely to invest in a community, particularly an economically weakened one, characterized by political conflict and scandal.

Throughout the 1950s, Elefante was recognized as a political force even beyond East Utica, and to no small extent his prominence related to the fact that he was a key leader in a relatively rare upstate Democratic stronghold. In 1950, *New York Times* political correspondent Warren Moscow published a study entitled *Politics in the Empire State* in which he characterized Utica and Oneida County as second in importance (after Albany County) among upstate Democratic centers. It should be remembered that this was a time in which a few thousand votes in upstate New York could help determine the fate of Democratic candidates for statewide office like Governor; indeed, in 1954, when Averell Harriman became the first Democrat to win the governorship since Dewey's election in 1942, his statewide margin of victory was a mere 11,000 votes.

In addition, Elefante's position as a leader among upstate Italians, one of the largest ethnic groups in New York, also enhanced his influence in state Democratic circles. In the mid-1950s, the Secretary of the State Democratic Committee characterized Elefante as "quite a powerful political figure upstate among the Italians." In 1954, the Italian Embassy asked Elefante to attend a reception, to which, in the words of the invitation, the "most highly representative Italian-Americans from all over the United States" had been invited. The next year, Governor Harriman invited Elefante to a luncheon reception in honor of the Italian Ambassador.

At the outset of the 1950s, the Utica newspapers were again becoming interested in Elefante. A generally thoughtful and marvelously detailed three-part series of articles written by *Observer-Dispatch* reporter David Beetle in the second half of 1949 helped to mark the renewal of journalistic interest in Elefante's role in local political life. Beetle's articles—which he wrote because, as he put it, "for years we've been hearing about how 'Rufe [sic] Elefante runs the city'"—said much about not only Elefante, but what many people outside of East Utica probably imagined him to be. Elefante, Beetle related, was not a shadowy figure—he was easily contacted, "neither dodged nor hesitated" in answering questions, had a good sense of humor, and was enviably dapper. In addition, his "English was good; his vocabulary amazingly wide." An implication of these observations was that readers might otherwise have assumed that East Uticans were graceless and inarticulate and that politicians like Elefante were crass, aggressive, or evasive. In contrast, it was clear that Beetle was impressed and even rather sympathetic to Elefante. Indeed, after noting that people could always organize politically and vote against a political organization like Elefante's if they "don't like the way a ward, a town, or a city is run," Beetle concluded that this was unlikely to happen in Utica because "we're too darned satisfied" with the way things were going.

Although the election returns suggested that Beetle's conclusion was justified, the newspapers that employed him were not quite so satisfied as were many Uticans. Throughout the 1950s, the Utica newspapers periodically published editorials contending that it was neither healthy nor proper for a small group of people, or a supposedly all-powerful political boss, to have so much influence over local government. In the second half of the 1950s, the papers became increasingly aggressive in taking this stand in dozens of articles and editorials that contended that businesses Elefante and his allies owned had profited either to an unseemly or improper extent in providing services to local government and that local government was lax in its response to other illicit activities in Utica.

In November 1957, at a tiny community called

Apalachin, the New York State Police raided what turned out to be a gathering of organized crime figures from throughout the United States. Among those netted were three men from East Utica. A reporter from the *New York Journal-American* visited Utica for approximately 48 hours, and on the basis of his visit, he wrote a series of highly sensationalistic articles in January 1958 that contended that Utica was an unusually corrupt, wide-open town in which vice ran rampant—supposedly so unique was the situation in Utica that it deserved, the author argued, to be called the "Sin City of the East," a ridiculous label that stuck, much to the detriment of local economic development efforts.

Elefante's opponents contended that Utica would not have been "sinful" if he had simply willed it to be otherwise. To this day, there is arguably no clear consensus on this contention; one can only make a few observations. Complaints about official tolerance of illicit activity had surfaced periodically in Utica since the late nineteenth century and as recently as the mid-1940s, when City Hall was in Republican hands. In addition, Republicans controlled City Hall in 1960-68 and "anti-Rufie" Democrats controlled it in 1968-72, and yet, when another outside journalist visited Utica in 1971, he found that, although vice was not so blatant as it may have once been, it was still found downtown. In addition, notwithstanding the decline of Elefante's power, organized crime was not eradicated from Utica until the mid-1980s, and then only after the aggressive intervention of the federal government. Such activity, in short, continued on some level for decades regardless of who controlled City Hall. In addition, as David Beetle predicted, and as the election results after 1959 demonstrated, Elefante could not retain power if voters were so dissatisfied with the machine's rule, and as some local reformers and even outsiders observed, before Apalachin much of the local public had known only too well what was going on in the midst of the county's principal commercial center, but they also chose to ignore it until it brought notoriety upon Utica.

In any case, exaggerated or not, justified or not, scandal and a series of investigations ensued into the early 1960s. Elefante was not among the dozen Uticans hauled before the legislature's "Watchdog Committee," which held the first public investigations into the Apalachin affair, but he testified before the Oneida County grand jury in April 1958, and in July 1959, he also appeared before the special grand jury led by special prosecutor Robert Fischer. On the latter occasion, Elefante dismissively tossed aside an offer of immunity and challenged the proceedings of the special grand jury in a letter he defiantly released to the local press. Elefante and his allies also fought back through surrogates, like a short-lived newspaper named The *Vanguard*, and local Italian American organizations, which complained to Governor Nelson Rockefeller that the investigations were fundamentally anti-Italian in motivation; Rockefeller was unmoved by such pleas.

After years of official and journalistic investigation, Elefante was not even indicted—let alone convicted—of wrong-doing, but he did not emerge unscathed. Although his political career continued into the 1980s, his reputation and the East Utica machine were damaged. Mayor John McKennan, the two-term Democratic incumbent, chose not to seek re-election and instead ran for city judge in 1959, and the Republican candidate, Frank Dulan, subsequently won the mayoralty, thus initiating an historically-long run of Republican rule at City Hall. Unfortunately for Utica, Dulan was unable to reenergize the "Loom to Boom" economic revival of the 1950s, because the scandal, and political warfare it had ignited, made the area seem much less appealing to potential employers than it had been to companies like General Electric, UNIVAC, the Chicago Pneumatic Tool Company, and Bendix prior to 1957-58.

In addition, amidst all the upheaval of the late 1950s, Elefante endured much personal sadness. His father, Pasquale, died in March 1959, and Rufie's wife of 32 years, the former Mary Zangrone, died in January 1960. In the course of less than a year, he had lost two of the most important people in his personal life—this at a time when he was already besieged by political difficulty. Elefante nevertheless battled on—indeed, in the 1960s, he became more openly aggressive in defying his critics and determined to keep his organization together despite the rise of challengers who were increasingly effective even within his long-time stronghold, East Utica.

1950's

Take Utica, For Instance . . .

It's a place where small businessmen sometimes grapple with big problems, and in a manner to suggest that the American way of life still has its practitioners.

by Robert Sheehan

THE BEST THINGS in life can be boring at times, and one of the Club's most popular members, Richard H. Balch, President of Horrocks-Ibbotson Co., fishing-tackle manufacturer, likes to vary the menu occasionally by strolling to lunch at a place called Marino's in the old and unfashionable part of town. The Horrocks-Ibbotson plant, too, is still located in the forsaken section of the city, hard by the route of the historic—and long since totally erased—Erie Canal. Like so many U.S. cities, as Utica grew and "progressed" it did not rebuild but simply moved on, leaving a number of its once-proud homes to deteriorate into slums or slovenly lofts. When he leaves his office Dick Balch usually ducks up a dilapidated alleyway and enters the rear of the Horrocks-Ibbotson retail sporting-goods store, which provides him with a short cut to lower Genesee Street. "This store," says Dick, "was established in 1812 and, if you don't believe it, just take a look at some of the merchandise." It is the store in which Dick Balch's grandfather, Hugh J. Horrocks, went to work as a clerk when he came over from England in 1863. Mr. Horrocks eventually bought into the firm and in 1895 started the manufacturing venture that has now become one of the largest and most enterprising firms of its kind in the world.

The route to Marino's leads across Genesee and down shabby Catherine Street, and along the way Dick will give his easy greeting to at least a dozen people, many of them in rough working clothes, and perhaps be stopped for a chat by one or two. At the restaurant he will pause to ask what's new of proprietor Frank Marino, who usually works the bar himself at noon, and then sit down to lunch with one of the frequenters—Charley Donnelly, the postmaster; Joe Davoli, educational director of the Textile Workers Union; or maybe the Great Dictator, Rufus Elefante himself. (The truth is Dick dabbles a bit in politics, and Democratic party politics, at that.) "What do your uptown friends think of your consorting with the boys at Marino's?" you ask Dick. He gives you a grin. "I think they think it's romantic," he says.

Excerpt from Fortune magazine's 1949 feature article praising Utica's economic renewal efforts.

UTICA DAILY PRESS

32 PAGES *The Home Newspaper for Utica and Vicinity* ★

VOL. LXVIII, NO. 256 UTICA, N. Y., FRIDAY MORNING, JANUARY 6, 1950 PRICE FIVE CENTS

Elefante Announces His Retirement as East Utica Leader

Marino's restaurant, onto which the Observer-Dispatch had mischievously superimposed a photo of the old City Hall tower, suggesting that Marino's was where power was really located in Utica.

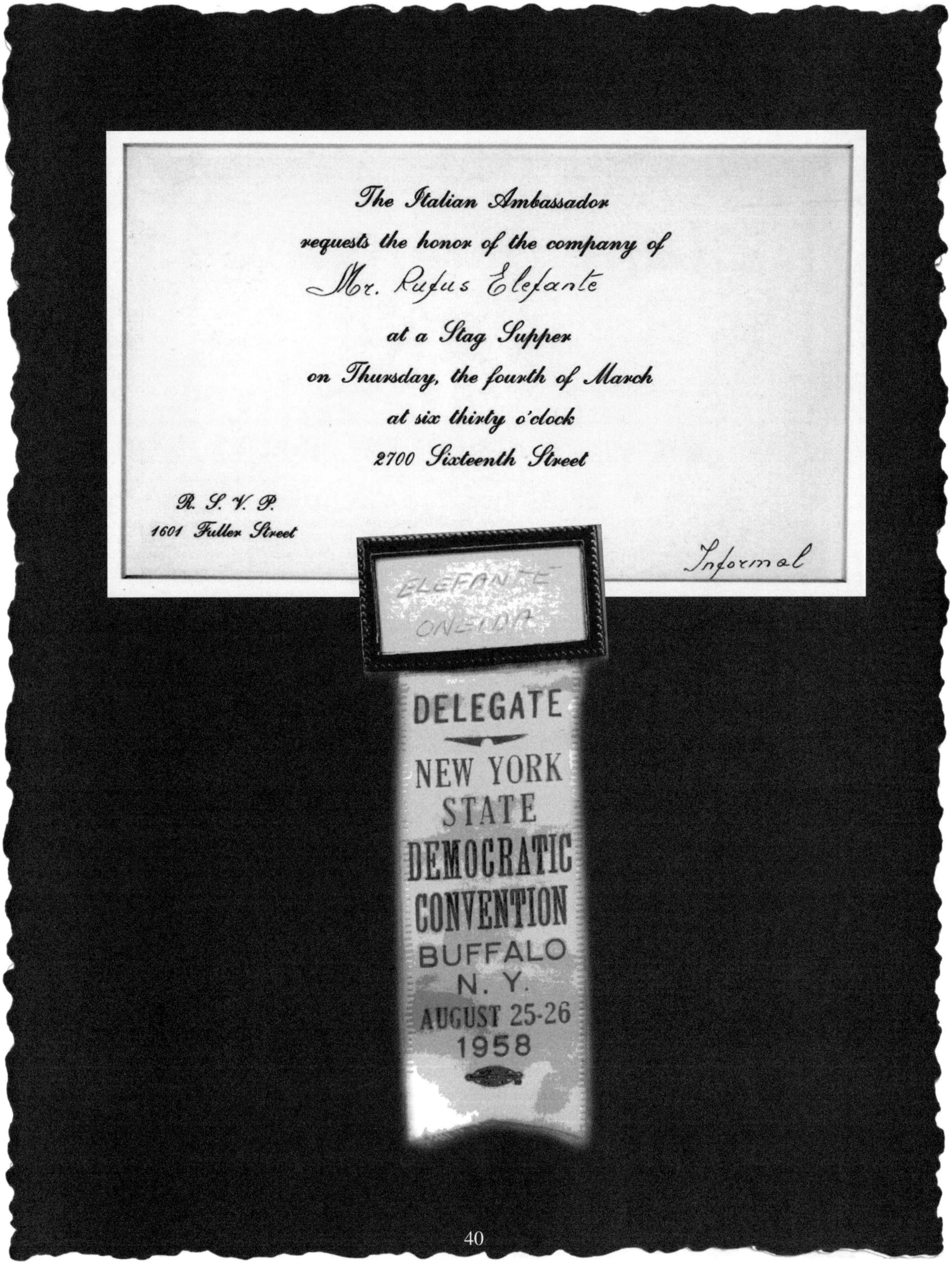
The Italian Ambassador
requests the honor of the company of
Mr. Rufus Elefante
at a Stag Supper
on Thursday, the fourth of March
at six thirty o'clock
2700 Sixteenth Street
R. S. V. P.
1601 Fuller Street
Informal
ELEFANTE
ONEIDA
DELEGATE
NEW YORK STATE DEMOCRATIC CONVENTION
BUFFALO N. Y.
AUGUST 25-26 1958

THE CONSUL GENERAL OF ITALY

690 PARK AVENUE
NEW YORK 21, N.Y.

Dear Mr.Elefante,

His Excellency the Italian Ambassador in Washington, Dr. Alberto Tarchiani, has asked me to convey to you his personal invitation to attend a reception thatwill be held at the Italian Embassy on Thursday, March the 4th, 1954 from 6 p.m., on the occasion of the constitution of the American Resettlement Council for Italian Refugees (A.R.C.I.R.).

Enclosed with H.E. the Ambassador's invitation you will find an Announcement explaining the aims and purposes of the ARCIR, as well as well as the Charter of this new and all-important organization that proposes to make possible, in close collaboration with the proper Authorities of the United States and Italy, the settlement, in this country, of the 45.000 Italian Refugees who are admitted pursuant to the Refugee Relief Act of 1953.

Invitations to the constituent meeting at the Italian Embassy have been restricted to a limited number of the most highly representative Italian-Americans from all over the United States. H.E. the Ambassador's invitation therefore represents a tribute to your particular merits in the field of work and social activity, and the pursuit of the noble aim that the ARCIR proposes to attain: namely, the furtherance of the major interests of the United States and Italy through the settlement in this country, during the next three years, of the 45.000 refugees admitted by the above-mentioned Law.

In carrying out the instructions of H.E. the Ambassador, I am pleased to assure you that your presence at the meeting of March 4th at the Italian Embassy in Washington shall be particularly appreciated by the Italian Government.

Due to the brief delay, I would be much obliged to you if you could signify your acceptance by letter or telegram addressed to the Consul General of Italy in New York, 690 Park Avenue.

I await your corteous acknowledgement, and, with kindest regards, I remain, dear Mr.Elefante,

Sincerely,

C de Ferrariis S.

Carlo de Ferrariis Salzano

Mr.Rufus Elefante
514 Broad Street
Utica, N.Y.

EXCELSIOR

Governor and Mrs. Averell Harriman

request the pleasure of

The Honorable and Mrs Rufus Elefante

company at Luncheon

on *Saturday, April the second*

at *one-fifteen* **o'clock**

To meet His Excellency, The Prime Minister of Italy and Signora Scelba

Grand Jurors Hear Rayhill And Elefante

Three witnesses, Rufus P. Elefante, Leo M. Rayhill and Detective John Belmont, yesterday answered subpoenas to appear before the extended Oneida Count Grand Jury, investigating vice and crime in Utica.

District Attorney John M. Liddy said the jury would continue in session today. It had been in recess for a week.

Elefante, a Utica Democratic leader, and Rayhill, Oneida County Republican chairman, appeared during the afternoon session. Belmont, suspended from the Police Department since March 19, appeared at the morning session.

Liddy refused to answer questions about the appearances of the two political leaders.

The Grand Jury investigation was launched after public hearings of the Legislature's Watchdog Committee and Acting State Investigation Commissioner Arthur L. Reuter had focused attention on the city.

Belmont was suspended by Safety Commissioner Boyd Golder on the request of Reuter, who said the Utica detective had refused to answer certain questions when he appeared before Reuter in New York.

Belmont was suspended without pay. Golder said yesterday there had been no developments in Belmont's case since this suspension.

In suspending Belmont, Golder said he had been informed by Reuter that the detective had not given satisifactory answers to some questions and refused to answer others about the investigation of police affairs in Utica.

Rufus P. Elefante, top left, a Democratic leader in Utica, waits near Oneida County grand jury room yesterday while Attorney Jacob Goldbas stands by.

July 16, 1959

Hon. Robert E. Fischer
Special Attorney General
Oneida County Investigation
Utica, New York

Dear Sir:

Pursuant to a subpoena, served by your office upon me, I appeared before the Extraordinary Grand Jury on the 10th day of July, 1959 at 1:30 P.M. Although your subpoena called for my appearance as a witness, at no time was an oath administered to me. I am also of the belief that the grand jury present lacked a legal quorum to function.

In view of the foregoing, I do not deem it necessary to make any decision now as to whether or not I shall execute the proferred limited waiver pursuant to Section 103B of the General Municipal Law which became effective July 1, 1959.

You are fully aware that my previous sworn testimony before this same grand jury disclosed that at no time did my firm have a contract with the City of Utica, County of Oneida or State of New York. I did testify that, in the unusual Winter of 1957, my firm was hired on an hourly basis along with many other firms for the removal of snow. My testimony clearly establishes that this snow removal was the only work my firm had with the City of Utica in the last eleven (11) years.

To avoid any misunderstanding, I cannot refrain from stating that henceforth if I am subpoenaed as a witness before the grand jury, I will immediately insist that the oath be administered as required by law.

Respectfully yours,

Rufus P. Elefante

Rufie: Never Had City Contract

RUFUS P. ELEFANTE

Rufus P. Elefante said last night that his firm, Elefante & Mazza, Inc., truckers, has never had a contract with the city.

The statement was made when the Democratic leader released a copy of a letter to Special Prosecutor Robert E. Fischer. The letter, dated July 16, explained why Elefante had not signed a waiver of immunity, when he appeared before the special grand jury recently.

Elefante's statement and letter came on the heels of an announcement by Fischer that Elefante's firm was one of five barred from city business for five years.

Fischer's action, barring the firms, was based on the refusal of nine of the firms' members to sign waivers of immunity. Elefante was not one of those listed. Instead, his firm was barred by the refusal of Peter Mazza, the firm's treasurer.

• • •

THE LETTER said Elefante had appeared before the jury on July 10, but "at no time was an oath administered to me."

"I am also of the belief that the grand jury present lacked a legal quorum to function," the letter continued.

"In view of the foregoing, I do not deem it necessary to make any decision now as to whether or not I shall execute the proffered limited waiver . . ." the letter said.

• • •

CITY-COUNTY REPORT

You Get a Stare, A Blank Look Or a Smile

By WILLIAM H. LOHDEN

"Did you lunch with Rufie during the Judicial Convention in Syracuse?" a delegate was asked.

"How do I know who I had lunch with?" he replied, laughing.

The "Rufie" mentioned obviously was Utica's Democratic boss, Rufus P. Elefante.

The response of the delegate, one of the city's leading Democrats, is typical of the reluctance found also among city officials, when it comes to talking about the "boss" or even mentioning his name.

●

Invariably, any reference in City Hall to Elefante or his activities brings a blank stare, feigned ignorance or just a wry smile.

Yet, as most know, in and out of the Hall, Elefante and his power are ever-present in the minds and actions of city officials. Although he rarely, if ever, makes an appearance at the Hall, frequent meetings are held elsewhere.

"His Nibs" or **"the Boss,"** as Elefante is called on occasions, is even said to "reign" at almost daily "court" sessions at Marino's Restaurant during lunch hour.

The royal inference indicates the high power Elefante is believed, or known, to exercise.

●

Those who wish an audience, but who are not members of the "royal court," may seek an appointment with Elefante at his deceptively unobtrusive office in the garage of Elefante & Mazza, 514 Broad.

"You've got to see Rufie," is still the half-joking reply to those who want things done in the city, although Elefante retired in 1950 from the only top official post. He had headed the East Utica Democratic Club since 1928.

In the future, he would be **"just an ordinary Democrat,"** Elefante, who is now 55, said on his retirement. He has, however, remained a member of the county Democratic Committee.

Although he has kept out of the limelight, the "boss" probably has grown in political stature.

●

His publicity shyness has added an air of mystery to the "boss" in the public's eye. The name "Rufie" at the same time has a magic quality. **It is a nickname as readily identified locally as "Ike" is internationally.**

In person and habits, Elefante belies his position. He is fairly short and stocky. His horned-rim glasses and average clothes give him the appearance of a typical successful businessman.

Elefante's unostentatious habits carry through to his car, an ordinary two-tone Chrysler sedan. Those who have heard of Elefante are surprised at his lack of pretentiousness when they meet him.

The legend which naturally goes with a mysterious political boss gives rise to countless rumors. Some say Elefante's power reaches far beyond the city, into Albany and possibly Washington.

Others claim he not only rules the city Democrats with an iron hand but that he is a strong power in Republican circles.

DEMOCRATIC STATE COMMITTEE
HOTEL SHERATON-TEN EYCK
ALBANY, NEW YORK

PHONE 5-6261

MICHAEL H. PRENDERGAST
CHAIRMAN

Dear Rufie:

I just learned of the death of your Father and I want you to know how sorry I was to hear the news.

Please be assured of a remembrance for your Father in my prayers.

With warm personal regards, I am

Sincerely,

Mike

Michael H. Prendergast
Chairman

Mr. Rufus Elefante
1601 Gibson Road
Utica, New York

April 1st, 1959

2-B—Observer-Dispatch Utica, Sun., Oct. 11, 1959

Hard-Driving Elefante Keeps Democrats on Toes

Party Runs Like An Oiled Machine

By WILLIAM LOHDEN

The Democratic Party here, unlike its opponent, runs like a well-oiled IBM machine. There may be chatterings, rumblings and occasional squawks, but they are rarely heard by the outsider.

The main reason for the party's unity and success is its leader, **Rufus P. Elefante,** who keeps party leaders toeing the line with his hard-driving, near dictatorial power.

The party enjoys a comfortable edge of about 9,000 votes in the city's total enrollment of more than 40,000. As a result, it has not been difficult to hold control of City Hall and the Common Council.

Officially, the party is controlled by a 26-member County executive committee, headed by Walter D. McIncrow, and the city committee, headed by Frank Emma.

These groups are little more than rubber stamps for Elefante, many high Democrats readily admit. Some officials, perhaps resentful of being little more than pawns, claim Elefante is not as all-powerful as most people believe.

• • •

THE SHORT, heavy-set leader reigns mostly at his trucking firm office, 514 Broad St. A number of persons are often seen waiting outside his office for an audience.

At other times, mostly at mealtime, Elefante confers with his aides at Marino's Restaurant, just a block from his office. In his explosive fashion, Elefante dictates orders and policy in minute detail.

He will listen and be influenced by his advisors when he does not have a decided opinion. But, most of Elefante's lieutenants wait for the "boss" to state an opinion, or ask for opinions of others

Rizzo: 'He'd Be Elected'

Rufie Gives the Word: 'I May Run for Mayor'

By TONY VELLA

Utica Democratic leader Rufus (Rufie) P. Elefante has fired the opening guns of the November municipal elections.

The word was sent out yesterday that Elefante is "seriously considering" running for mayor.

There was immediate speculation that Elefante is attempting to determine the public's attitude toward the Democratic organization in view of the current state-ordered probe of vice and crime in Utica.

• • •

THE REPORT of his possible candidacy sent political observers searching for the significance of what appeared to be a move to shock Democrats out of a pessimistic attitude caused by the probe.

If Elefante does run in November, it would be one of the biggest political surprises in years. It would be a complete departure from his role as a behind-the-scenes king maker.

There were some who doubted that Elefante will make the mayoral run. They regarded Elefante's move strictly as a trial balloon.

• • •

WHEN SEVERAL of Elefante's close associates were letting out the word of his possible candidacy yesterday, they suggested that he could roll up a huge victory margin at the polls because of a large personal following.

The report also may have been designed to bolster Democrats throughout the city, many who admittedly fear the possibility losing in November as the result of Special Prosecutor Robert E. Fischer's current probe.

Talk of Elefante's possible candidacy apparently is designed to reveal how much and what kind of backing the Democratic organization will receive during the campaign.

RUFUS ELEFANTE

DRAFT

RUFUS P.

ELEFANTE

for

MAYOR

City of Utica

17

LET'S NOT USE A GREATER UTICA . . . BUT BUILD A GREATER UTICA.

The VANGUARD

FOR UTICA-ROME AND ONEIDA COUNTY **5¢**

VOL. I NO. 4 (Weekly) October 9, 1959

Federation of Italian-American Societies

APPEAL TO GOVERNOR— END SPECIAL INVESTIGATION

Federation of Italian-American Societies
UTICA, NEW YORK

OFFICERS

Charles G. Merlini, *President*
Vito DeSantis, *First Vice-President*
Joseph Traversa, *Second Vice-President*
Thomas Landolfi, *Third Vice-President*
Beatrice DeSantis, *Treasurer*
Eugenio Petrucci, *Secretary*

SPECIAL COLUMBUS DAY COMMITTEE

Frank Dardano, *Assistant Treasurer*
Thomas Landolfi, *Tickets*
Marchesa Di Seravalle, *Publicity*

The VANGUARD

FOR UTICA-ROME AND ONEIDA COUNTY **5¢**

VOL. I, NO. 3 (Weekly) October 2, 1959

SONS OF ITALY FOR JUSTICE — AGAINST DISCRIMINATION

An Open Letter To Gov. NELSON ROCKEFELLER:

This is the text of a letter written and approved by the members of the Sons of Italy. The original copy of this letter was sent to Governor Nelson Rockefeller.

September 30, 1959

THE HONORABLE NELSON D. ROCKEFELLER
GOVERNOR, THE STATE OF NEW YORK
State Capitol Building
Albany I, New York

Dear Governor:

We, the members of the Utica Lodge No. 2054, Order Sons of Italy in America, have this day passed unanimously a resolution requesting that the Governor of New York State look into the special investigation presently being con-

— city employee has been accused of pilfering $900.00 worth of lumber!

There is but little doubt that former Governor Harriman ordered this investigation for political purposes only. We know that you, Governor Rockefeller, would never have done so. The people of Italian extraction in Utica, who happen to be predominantly Democrat, voted overwhelmingly for you, a Republican, perhaps because of your liberal background and your sympathy for minority groups of all nationalities.

We implore you to use your office — and your heart — to put a stop to headline persecution born out of hate and

The 1960s

Despite the challenges Elefante faced at the outset of the 1960s, the *Observer-Dispatch* contended that the Democratic organization still ran "like an oiled machine," and in a mischievous moment, Elefante suggested he might defy his critics by running for mayor. In June 1960, he released yet another of his retirement announcements, which predictably elicited skepticism. Even after the upsets of the preceding years, it seemed conceivable that Elefante might soon rebuild his political fortunes. In July 1960, he headed to Los Angeles to attend the Democratic National Convention. After casting a ballot for Lyndon Johnson for the presidential nomination, Elefante eventually threw his support behind John F. Kennedy. Although he was invited to Kennedy's Inauguration and was one of the official vice chairmen of the Democratic State Committee Victory Dinner at the Waldorf in February 1961, Elefante's relationship with the Kennedys, particularly the President's brother Bobby, became increasingly cool as the 1960s progressed.

Elefante—specifically, whether one was "for" or against him—became a perennial local political issue from the late 1950s until the early 1980s, and however influential he remained, he persistently failed to find a successful mayoral candidate until the 1970s. In 1961 Frank Dulan made history by becoming the first Republican ever to be re-elected mayor of Utica; Dulan was re-elected to two more terms, in 1963 and 1965, sweeping aside both machine candidates and, at first, reform candidates, most notably Dominick Assaro and the movement he, local lawyer Fred Nassar, and *Observer-Dispatch* reporter William Lucy built in the middle years of the decade.

Arguably the high point of Elefante's campaign to regain the political initiative and to fire up his historical base was a banquet in 1962, attended by a thousand local machine loyalists, at which the guest of honor was Carmine DeSapio, the recently overthrown National Democratic Committeeman and one-time New York State kingmaker. Reformers sought a court injunction to halt the event, contending that Elefante had no right to sponsor a "Democratic Party" event, but Elefante mockingly, and successfully, dismissed these efforts by contending that the "East Utica Democratic organization," not the party, was its sponsor. Elefante went on to deliver a speech at the dinner in which he proudly summarized the accomplishments of his organization and essentially dismissed as insignificant what all other local leaders had accomplished.

Local reformers increasingly allied with Bobby Kennedy, who was elected to represent New York in the United States Senate in 1964. Kennedy had Elefante's support in 1964, but he and the new Senator and their respective local supporters increasingly came to loggerheads. New York City Mayor Robert Wagner, the de facto leader of the state's Democrats in the immediate aftermath of DeSapio's downfall, came up to Utica in 1964 in an effort to bring peace to what had been one of New York's few Democratic strongholds west of the Hudson. However, Wagner's efforts, and those of others, to heal the breach among local Democrats came to nothing.

With the political cold war between Elefante's supporters and Bobby Kennedy's local allies becoming increasingly hot, Elefante made every effort to prevent the election of Dominick Assaro, a former Republican who ran for Mayor as a Democrat with Kennedy's active backing in 1967. Elefante went on television and radio and blanketed East Utica with fliers. By every means possible, he called upon local voters, most specifically those in East Utica, to reject "outside interference" in Utica's political life. Indeed, Elefante condemned Kennedy and the young Senator's allies as anti-Italian.

However, Rufie's efforts were to no avail in the short run, as Assaro won the mayoralty in 1967 and was re-elected in 1969. As the 1960s drew to a close, Elefante's prospects for a full comeback seemed to be dimming. Nevertheless, during the next decade, his career was again on the upswing, and however brief Elefante's later political renaissance was, it bore testimony to his unusual staying power as a local political leader.

1960's

Utica, Sunday, June 26, 1960 Observer-Dispatch—3-B

CITY-COUNTY REPORT

Elefante's Latest 'Retirement' Finds Some Skepticism

By WILLIAM LOHDEN

Rufus P. Elefante has cried "wolf" too often for people to believe he is really retiring from politics.

"Oh, he has said that so many times, who's going to believe it?" was a typical response to the veteran leader's retirement from the Democratic county executive committee.

It seems that about every decade, Elefante, for one reason or another, has announced he was retiring from an active political role.

• • •

A YEAR ago, when the Democrats seemed at a loss as to how they were going to overcome two years of bad publicity and win the November city election, Elefante supposedly "leaked" a story that he was considering running for mayor.

Not too many took the report seriously. Some of Elefante's aides said at the time he was just sending up a trial balloon on his popularity of the moment.

The balloon apparently came crashing down, and again Elefante announced he was retiring. Some close to him say he did retire to a degree last year.

Now, it looks like there may be more truth to his retirement than ever before. With Elefante, top aides Dennis P. O'Dowd and Charles S. Donnelly also have retired from the execuitve committee.

• • •

AFTER the drubbing the local Democrats have taken in the past two years from three state investigations, the loss of the city election last fall, and the ominous Republican upheaval in the primary, it is no wonder the Democrats have decided to act.

Younger party leaders have indicated that the days of the "boss" type of party rule have become outmoded. They feel party strategy should be more subtle and based less on personality.

STATE OF NEW YORK

DEPARTMENT OF STATE

I Hereby Certify that the party position described below was uncontested at the Primary Election held in this State on the 7th day of June 1960, and as a result, Rufus P. Elefante was duly elected, without balloting, DISTRICT DELEGATE TO THE DEMOCRATIC NATIONAL CONVENTION FROM THE Thirty-fourth CONGRESSIONAL DISTRICT.

Witness my hand and seal of office at the City of Albany, this 24th day of June, 1960.

CAROLINE K. SIMON,
Secretary of State

by: ROBERT D. STONE
Executive Deputy Secretary of State

United States Senate
WASHINGTON, D.C.

August 12, 1960

Honorable Rufus P. Elefante
1601 Gibson Road
Utica, New York

Dear Rufe:

On my return to Washington I want to take this time to thank you for your vote of confidence in Los Angeles.

I am looking forward to seeing you again and working with you during the crucial months ahead. With your support I know we will accomplish our purpose.

I am sending under separate cover a copy of my acceptance speech.

With every good wish, I am

Sincerely,

John F. Kennedy

JFK:lbf

INAUGURATION OF PRESIDENT AND VICE PRESIDENT
KENNEDY JOHNSON

The Inaugural Committee

requests the honor of your presence
to attend and participate in the Inauguration of

John Fitzgerald Kennedy

as President of the United States of America
and

Lyndon Baines Johnson

as Vice President of the United States of America
on Friday the twentieth of January
one thousand nine hundred and sixty-one
in the City of Washington

Edward H. Foley
Chairman

Victory Dinner

Democratic State Committee of New York

Saturday Evening, February 11, 1961

Waldorf-Astoria

CHAIRMAN	CO-CHAIRMAN	HONORARY CHAIRMAN
EUGENE J. KEOGH	MRS. LOUIS S. GIMBEL, JR.	ARTHUR LEVITT

VICE CHAIRMEN

ADDABBO, JOSEPH P.	GEROSA, LAWRENCE E.	PIKE, OTIS G.
ANFUSO, VICTOR L.	GILBERT, JACOB H.	POWELL, ADAM CLAYTON, JR.
BARBARITA, FRANK R.	GOLDWATER, MONROE	QUILLINAN, FRANCIS J.
BOTWINICK, BENJAMIN	GUREVICH, ABRAHAM J.	ROONEY, JOHN J.
BRAGALINI, GEORGE M.	HARRIMAN, AVERELL	ROSENDALE, WILLIAM A.
BRANDT, HARRY	HEALEY, JAMES C.	RUGGIERI, BERNARD J.
BROWN, PETER CAMPBELL	HOLTZMAN, LESTER	RYAN, AILEEN B.
BOYLE, THOMAS F.	KELLY, DAVID W.	RYAN, WILLIAM FITTS
BUCHANAN, BESSIE	KELLY, EDNA F.	SANTANGELO, ALFRED E.
BUCKLEY, CHARLES A.	KELLY, WILLIAM A.	SEDITA, FRANK A.
CAREY, HUGH L.	LOUGHLIN, EDWARD V.	SHALLECK, MILTON
CELLER, EMANUEL	LYNCH, THOMAS	SHANAHAN, THOMAS J.
CLEMENTE, L. GARY	MARTONE, ANGELO J.	SMITH, JOHN J.
COLE, THOMAS	McFADDEN, JAMES J.	SOUHAN, FRANCIS J.
COLEMAN, JOHN A.	McGRATH, JOHN P.	STARK, ABE
CROTTY, PETER J.	McKEON, WILLIAM H.	STEVENSON, JOHN
DELANEY, JAMES J.	MERKIN, MICHAEL J.	STRATTON, SAMUEL S.
DOWNEY, MORTON J.	MILBURN, DEVEREUX	TIERNEY, FRANCIS J.
DUKE, ANGIER BIDDLE	MORGAN, WILLIAM H.	TRAVIA, ANTHONY J.
DULSKI, THADDEUS J.	MULTER, ABRAHAM J.	UCHITEL, MAURICE
ELEFANTE, RUFUS	MURPHY, JAMES K.	VOLET, WILLIAM B.
FARBSTEIN, LEONARD	MURRAY, THOMAS E., JR.	YOUNG, JOHN
FARLEY, JAMES A.	NACHTMAN, PAUL	ZARETZKI, JOSEPH
GAMBINO, SALVATORE T.	NOVA, BARNETT J.	ZECK, WILLIAM A.
GARRITY, HAROLD T.	O'BRIEN, LEO W.	ZELENKO, HERBERT

Executive Coordinator — MORTON SUNSHINE

★

OFFICERS OF THE DEMOCRATIC STATE COMMITTEE OF NEW YORK

MICHAEL H. PRENDERGAST, *Chairman*
MAE GUREVICH, *Vice Chairman*
CARMINE G. DeSAPIO, *National Committeeman*
EDNA F. KELLY, *National Committeewoman*
RAYMOND C. DEERING, *Treasurer*
BENJAMIN WETZLER, *Secretary*
MONROE GOLDWATER, *Chairman of the Law Committee*

Elefante Defies Party Reformers

RUFUS ELEFANTE
'I'll Run Meetings'

By LAURENCE PAUL

Democratic kingpin Rufus P. Elefante hurled a challenge at reform leaders of the Democratic party last night when he vowed to direct future party meetings in East Utica.

Elefante, leader of the Old Guard wing of the party here, made his remarks after a closed meeting, which he said he had scheduled for Democratic workers in East Utica.

Asked if he ran the meeting, Elefante said he did, adding:

"And I'm going to run every other future one in East Utica, too."

County Democratic Chairman Lawrence T. Gilroy Jr., said last night the meeting called by Elefante was not official so far as the party was concerned.

Alfred Mirante, Democratic city chairman, could not be reached for comment.

Prior to 1961, the Republicans never managed to win two consecutive mayoral elections in Utica. Dulan's victories in the 1960s demonstrated that earlier accusations that Elefante was all-powerful were grossly exaggerated. The machine won before 1959 to no small extent because it was popular.

UTICA, N. Y., WEDNESDAY EVENING, NOVEMBER 8, 1961 — TELEPHONE SW 7-1111 — PRICE SEVEN CENTS

Dulan's Big Victory Signals An End to Elefante's Power

By TONY VELLA

The victory of Republican Mayor Frank M. Dulan may have dealt the death blow to the once-powerful Democratic organization in Utica.

Dulan's history-making win probably signalled the start of an upheaval in the hierarchy of the 30-year-old Democratic organization.

Some political observers said it might have spelled the end of the political career of Rufus P. Elefante, who for many years was the dominant figure and king-maker in the organization.

• • •

UNTIL YESTERDAY, the Elefante-led Democrats had never lost two consecutive municipal elections. Until yesterday, no Republican mayor had won two terms in succession.

Even in its few defeats on the mayoral level over the years, the organization had never lost control of the Common Council, as it did yesterday.

Democratic loyalists applauding Rufie in 1962. Beatrice (Bea) DeSantis, Deputy City Treasurer and Vice President of the East Utica Democratic Club, is third from left.

Rufie Puts Off Democratic Feud

By LAURENCE PAUL

Rufus P. Elefante announced last night he planned "to delay our intraparty fight with the present leadership" of the Oneida County Democratic organization until after the Nov. 6 election.

Elefante, old-line Democratic leader, said his decision for a moratorium was made "in order not to interfere with the chances of electing Democratic candidates this fall."

Reading from a prepared text, Elefante spoke to an estimated 200 East Utica Democratic workers who then praised his leadership and gave him a standing ovation. The open meeting was held in Hotel Hamilton.

• • •

LONG A POWERFUL although backstage figure in city and county politics, Elefante defended his type of leadership and assailed that of the reform party elements.

He attacked City Chairman Alfred Mirante. He called Lawrence T. Gilroy, reform chairman of the Oneida County Democratic Committee, a "Dulan Democrat" — a reference to Republican Mayor Frank M. Dulan.

He accused Gilroy and other reformers of bringing about "the re-election of the present Republican city administration" last fall.

He charged that "the reform group wants nothing less than to be the bosses."

• • •

AFTER THE MEETING, Elefante declined "at this time" to elaborate on his statement, concerning his future course of action with relation to the party.

He refused to say whether by declaring a moratorium on an intraparty skirmish he intended to support the re-election of Gilroy and Mirante to their present party offices.

He refused to say whether he would support Thomas J. Welch as the Democratic candidate for the new office of county executive.

• • •

NUMEROUS VETERAN PARTY stalwarts and Democratic public officials from East Utica attended and sat with Elefante at the head table.

But Councilman Louis F. Tomaino, Democratic minority leader in the Common Council, was absent. Tomaino represents East Utica's Seventh Councilmanic District.

Contacted at home after the meeting, Tomaino said: "I was not asked or invited to attend the meeting. I was under the impression that it was held for committeemen. I am not a committeeman, and not having been invited, I did not attend."

• • •

ELEFANTE SEEMED INTENT on dispelling the image of himself as a shadowy, behind-the-scenes power.

"During the years," he said at one point, "I've stayed in the background because I never wanted public office."

He said he never got a city, state or federal contract.

"I'm an ordinary man," he said near the end of the half-hour meeting.

• • •

AFTER ELEFANTE OPENED the meeting by reading his prepared remarks, several Democrats at the head table praised him in brief statements. Councilman Frank V. Andrello, D-6th District, for example, said he was "overwhelmed by Mr. Elefante's speech."

Gerald F. Donovan, unsuccessful candidate for mayor against Dulan last fall, advised the audience to "stick together and support our leader in years to come."

Donovan said he had been "affiliated" with Elefante for 30 years.

Others who spoke briefly were Supervisors Samuel D. Vatalaro, D-14th Ward, Ernest S. Marasco, D-15th Ward, Nicholas A. Colucci, D-16th Ward, and Councilman Fred Trino, D-8th District.

Sitting at the head table were Trino, Andrello, Marasco, Donovan, Vatalaro, Colucci and Nicholas Rizzo, an Elefante aide.

• • •

ELEFANTE COMMENTED on a number of things he had remained silent about for years.

Referring to the just-concluded special state investigation of vice and crime in Oneida County, he said:

"Evidently the method of state investigation is the new way of smashing the strength of a political party. The City of Utica has no more or less crime than any other city its size."

As for his style of leadership, he said:

"The fact that for 35 years, it was a unified organization and enjoyed continuous success at the polls speaks for itself."

On bossism, a charge often leveled at him, Elefante said this was "always the political cry of the 'outs' against the 'ins.'"

He added that "the back room in the past has been filled with the present members of the reform element."

• • •

REFERRING TO AN EDITORIAL in the Press that was critical of his leadership, Elefante said:

"I stand for that way when the word of a leader was his bond. I stand for the belief that leaders should refuse to hold public office or accept city contracts in order to protect and insure the success of his party at the polls. I stand for practical leadership and for organized party politics because I believe that political parties cannot function and have never functioned except with disastrous consequences without them."

UTICA DAILY PRESS

Utica, Friday, Sept. 14, 1962 Page 1

Elefante (left) Addresses East Utica Democrats

. . . Supervisors Vatalaro, Marasco, Councilman Trino

Walter McIncrow, Frank Emma, Jimmy Ricco, Carmine DeSapio, Carmen Paciccia, Rufie

Thank You, Mr. Elefante

Those who have fought and worked for good government and a strong two-party system in Utica and Oneida County have reason to be grateful to Rufus P. Elefante for the speech he made at his big dinner in the Hamilton Tuesday night.

Here, from the "boss" himself, was an admission of the existence of invisible government that went into action to get things done.

Here, from the man who personifies what he terms the "East Utica organization," was the arrogant claim that his organization was responsible for just about every progressive achievement in the city or county in the last 30 years.

* * *

IGNORED IN this paean of self-praise were the mayors and other elected officials and the countless other individuals and organizations that worked to bring the Rome air base to Oneida County, to establish Mohawk Valley Technical Institute, to improve streets, parks and playgrounds, to get arterial highways, an auditorium, urban renewal and other things the community needed.

The picture is clear that to get something done the thing to do was to "see Rufie." For Rufie, under the old system, controlled the aldermen and in some instances the mayors.

And this sort of thing we assume, came under the heading of what the speaker termed "democracy in action."

* * *

BUT IT IS not the voting public's idea of democracy. And that is precisely the reason, in our opinion, why the voters in 1959 began throwing the old crowd out. It is precisely the reason the Democratic party in Oneida County had to be reorganized.

In this speech we heard about the poor and downtrodden who eked out an existence via menial jobs distributed among them by this benevolent leader. But we heard nothing about the coterie of contractors and suppliers allied with his organization who grew fat and rich on profits from these great projects.

We heard about slums and slum clearance, but nothing about the slum landlords who profit from the new slums.

"We believe," said Mr. Elefante, "that government must be tolerant of human weakness; that government must govern with a heart."

* * *

IF "HUMAN WEAKNESS" is intended to cover prostitution, gambling, and stealing and corruption within a city administration, it is well that we now have a government that is less tolerant.

If governing with a heart means a government that closes its eyes to faithlessness and corruption among its police, it is well that we now have a government that is relatively heartless.

We heard, too, of "fair play." Does this include the civil service abuses that were common in the old days—the vote-buying, the political re-zonings, the welfare, hospitalization and public housing "arrangements?"

* * *

YES, MR. ELEFANTE, "the political sun still rises in the East," but it shines upon enlightened citizens, who have had enough of your kind of leadership, who have said so twice in municipal elections and who, in our opinion, will say so again and again, if necessary.

HICKORY HILL
4700 CHAIN BRIDGE ROAD
McLEAN, VIRGINIA

May 2, 1962

Dear Angela:

Many thanks at this late date for your letter explaining the situation involving you, your sister and the Post Office Department. I have passed your message along to my husband but you should not worry about any remarks which might have been made to him in Utica about your father.

I have also contacted someone in the Post Office Department about the garage and I hope everything will work out satisfactorily.

It was good to hear from you after all these years.

Sincerely,

Ethel Kennedy

Mrs. Robert F. Kennedy

Dr. Angela M. Elefante
1601 Gibson Road
Utica, New York

As early as 1962, as this letter from Ethel Kennedy suggests, Rufie was already becoming concerned about the intentions of the Kennedy family toward his organization.

Our Elefante Editorial Hit

OUR LOGIC - LACKING editorialist, who has a propensity for making his personal opinions sound like fact, expresses his amazement at the "effrontery" of Rufus P. Elefante for crediting the East Utica Democrat Organization with most of the progress achieved in Utica and Oneida County.

For years this editor has tagged Mr. Elefante with the "boss" label, and has steadfastly maintained his conviction that "Elefante was the man to see". He has accused Mr. Elefante of condoning — and even fostering — virtually all of the "evil doings" in City Hall.

Mr. Editor: If, as you insist, Mr. Elefante was the absolute "boss" who condoned and/or fostered Utica's sins, doesn't it follow that he must have been the "boss", or driving force, behind Utica's progress as well?

I realize(Mr. Editor, that any admission by you that Mr. Elefante might just possibly have been responsible for a small part of our community's progress would remove some of the tar and pitch from the image of this man which you have been laboring to create for so many years; nevertheless, won't you concede that Mr. Elefante cannot be "all-bad" any more than you yourself can be "all-good"?

AURELIO J. BIANCO
1130 Columbus Ave.

Editorial Page . . . Utica Observer-Dispatch — Wednesday, Nov. 6, 1963

A Diluted Victory

Many Dissatisfied

Mayor Dulan has achieved a third consecutive term, something new for Republican candidacies for that office.

He had a margin of more than 2,000 votes, comfortably higher than has decided many a mayoral election here. It is a great personal victory, but it is severely diluted by Democratic majority votes for other offices.

This is a tribute to the independence, if not always the judgment, of the voters. The margin of victory for the Mayor is about the same number of votes by which his fellow GOP candidates for assessorship lost their races. The swing of the voter from party to party was notable in other contests also.

The change of the Common Council majority to Democratic by one vote from its present alignment of Republicans by the same edge brings a Democrat, Thomas Durr, to office from the 2nd District. He has been independent of the Elefante machine. It could be worse.

Behemoth Roars Again

Our "Behemoth of Holy Writ" exults once more at re-election of Mayor Dulan and the passage of the assessor modernization program. This animal, lone survivor of a fire destroying the Utica Observer plant in 1884, traditionally howls again when happy even amid some disappointments at election time.

Frank Emma, Rufie, New York City Mayor Robert Wagner, Richard Balch

Nick Rizzo, Frank Andrello, Rufie, Sam Vatalaro

Jerry Fiore, Rufie, Jack Durant and the camera crew from WKTV at Rufie's house

OD Nov 1, 1965

3 Mayoral Rivals Say They're Confident

Elefante Tells East Utica: 'Assaro Has to Lose'

Democratic Leader Rufus P. Elefante issued a last minute appeal today for East Utica support of E. Vincent Eichler as all three camps headed into tomorrow's mayoral election saying they were confident of victory.

In a letter apparently sent to many East Utica Democrats, Elefante clearly reflected the Democratic fear of Dominick Assaro's estimated East Utica strength.

Strangely and remarkably, Elefante's approach was the same as Republican Mayor Dulan's: "Assaro cannot win."

Elefante said, therefore, "any vote you cast for him will not only be a lost vote, but will be a vote for Mayor Dulan."

Dulan contends that a vote for Independent-Liberal Assaro is a vote for Eichler.

• • •

EAST UTICA IS THE DEMOCRATIC fortress and is ethnically Italian. Assaro is expected to do better there than anywhere else.

The Assaro camp thinks he'll do well enough city-wide to become the first independent mayoral winner in a century.

Robert Steinhorst, an Assaro campaign manager, predicted an Assaro victory, sticking with the previously announced analysis that showed Assaro could win by this count: Assaro, 15,420; Dulan, 14,662, and Eichler, 12,182.

Neither major party however gives Assaro much of a chance.

City Republican Chairman Lawrence A. Tumposky sees it this way: Dulan, 21,000; Eichler, 15,000, and Assaro, 6,000.

Democratic City Chairman Alfred Mirante forecasts: Eichler, 19,500; Dulan, 14,000, and Assaro, 4,000.

Dulan commented: "I feel as though the people supported me for the last six years and, with the exception of a few, are still with me." He said he'd be trying to beat his 8,000-plus plurality of 1961.

Assaro said he was providing the people with a third choice. "The decision rests with all of the voters. I have complete confidence in the voters."

Eichler was reported out campaigning and not available for comment.

• • •

ALL THREE CANDIDATES will take to television tonight to wind up their campaigns. The Democrats held their last rally yesterday at Polonia Hall in East Utica.

Dulan forces hold a final rally tonight at the Tracy Restaurant on Tracy Street. Assaro regulars will conclude the campaign at his Genesee Street headquarters.

The polls open at 6, close at 9. More than 40,000 expected to vote.

UTICA DAILY PRESS

Page 9

Thursday, Dec. 30, 1965

RUFUS P. ELEFANTE

Report Rufie To Retire Draws Blast

Reports that Rufus P. Elefante might withdraw from Utica Democratic politics were greeted with skepticism in some quarters last night.

"The only time Elefante will retire is when he's in the grave," said James S. Kelly.

• • •

KELLY, the campaign manager in the Democratic mayoral campaign in 1963, later became disillusioned with the city organization dominated by Elefante.

"Any leader who would emerge from a so-called Elefante retirement would be a mere front," said Kelly.

There have been reports Elefante has called, or plans to call, a meeting of East Utica Democratic committeemen shortly after the New Year to announce his retirement.

• • •

ELEFANTE had no comment on these reports.

There have been moves

Press 3/11/66

Burns Draws Committee's Criticism; Elefante Praised

By LAURENCE J. PAUL

DEFENSE RESTS . . . Trio of Democratic leaders here defended local organization against state-level criticism. Alfred Mirante, standing, city chairman, said he had "taken all I can and all I will." At left, County Chairman G. Carl Morse; next to him, Benny Niles.

State Democratic Chairman John J. Burns was sharply criticized and Rufus P. Elefante was warmly praised last night at a meeting of the City Democratic executive committee.

City Chairman Alfred Mirante called Burns a "liar" and suggested he "go up and clean up his own county (Broome)."

Another executive committee member, Benny Niles, said Elefante, long-time Democratic power here, had been subjected to countless investigations and "he's come off as clean as a hound's tooth."

These comments were pieces of political shrapnel still spinning outward from the now-famous, shouted exchange in Albany on Feb. 26 between Mirante and Burns after a state meeting of Democratic county chairmen.

• • •

BURNS reportedly told Mirante that no one "closely associated" with Elefante would get a state patronage job.

"I did not go down there for patronage or anything else," Mirante said at one point last night. "He's a liar on that."

Mirante said he went to the meeting as a guest of County Chairman G. Carl Morse, that after the meeting he went "hat in hand" to discuss local party rumblings with Burns and "he gave me some very bad, foul name-calling." It was then, and only then, that Mirante replied in anger, the city chairman said.

An aide of Burns had "begged" Mirante, he continued, not to make public statements about the exchange. Mirante said he didn't mention it until called by a newspaper reporter after the story broke.

Mirante said he had "taken all I can and all I will in the future."

"I'm serving notice on Mr. Burns that his leadership is not of such a high standard. . . If he is a Democrat, then I don't want to be such a Democrat," Mirante said.

He suggested that Burns return to help "clean up his own county" and the City of Binghamton, where, Mirante added, news stories quoted the present mayor suggesting an investigation of a $700,000 deficit in city government spending. Burns is the immediately former mayor of Binghamton.

• • •

MIRANTE also attacked State Assemblyman Edward A. Hanna, D-Utica, and the Oneida County JFK Democratic Club. He called club members "Dulan Democrats." Dulan is Frank M. Dulan, the Republican mayor here.

Their club name, said Mirante, "cannot erase the treasonable acts they committed not only against the Democratic Party but against the people of Utica as a whole."

County Chairman Morse, however, gave cautious approval to the JFK Club at the same meeting.

Morse called the club members' intentions "honorable" and said he was confident members "will be good Democrats."

Niles said the leadership represented by Burns in the party was interested only in changing the guard locally, in substituting one dictator for another.

"If Elefante is a dictator," said Niles, "I'll make the best of it—because I know him."

Some members broke into applause at this statement.

• • •

MIRANTE blocked a suggestion that the committee go on record demanding an apology from Burns.

Earlier in the meeting, a discussion of Dulan's proposed budget of nearly $10 million occurred and Mirante appointed a subcommittee, headed by Robert Hammond, to review it and make recommendations. It was also pointed out that 22 of 24 members signed a resolution supporting the city party leadership at its last meeting.

Press 4/7/66

Rufie's Retirement Signal For Party Revitalization

Rufus P. Elefante has told Democratic members in the city that he is retiring.

He probably means it, although some, both friend and foe, are saying that the announcement must be a mistake, that this man, who has been a power in Democratic politics for 40 years, must be resorting to some kind of trickery.

But Mr. Elefante seldom said things he did not mean, especially in writing over his own name. His statement of retirement was made in personal letters to all of the party's 62 committee members in the city.

Rufus Elefante

* * *

MR. ELEFANTE is too well informed, too hard-nosed about his politics not to be aware that the string is running out. His Utica leadership and his influence in Oneida County Democratic politics has been repudiated by the New York State Democratic leadership. The feeling of insurgency against his leadership is strong—although not firmly organized — in the city and county.

Last November's city election was the fourth consecutive vote in which an Elefante-backed Democratic candidate was defeated for mayor, the office that had been for a quarter century the heart of Democratic power in the city and county. And, mostly significantly of all, Mr. Elefante's ability to get and give jobs, state and local—the lifeline of any political leader—has disappeared.

* * *

THE LATE M. William (Bill) Bray, the local Democratic boss, who rose to the lieutenant governorship in the 1930s, gave Mr. Elefante his first political post in 1923 when he was designated as the party's organization representative in East Utica. He was then 20.

Now, 43 years later, Mr. Elefante says he is quitting his East Utica leadership. Of course, political retirement does not mean political interment—especially after a grip that has lasted four decades. Mr. Elefante's counsel will be sought. What he says will continue to carry major weight. When East Utica Democrats pick a new leader, he will be an Elefante man.

* * *

BUT MR. ELEFANTE'S letter should be an invitation to Utica and Oneida County Democrats to reform their ranks, to seek out new leadership, to forget factions and find a new sense of direction.

This should not be a time for area Democrats to say this cannot be. This should be a time for the sunshine of reorganization and revitalization to remove the chill that Mr. Elefante has been imparting to Democratic progress in recent years.

EAST UTICA DEMOCRATIC ORGANIZATION
UTICA, NEW YORK

My Dear Fellow Democrats:

In tomorrow's election, you will go to the polls and decide the future of the Democratic Party in the County, in the City and especially East Utica.

For the past 40 years, the East Utica Democratic Organization has been the strength and political power for the people of East Utica.

Since the Kennedy's have ascended to political power and particularly Bobby Kennedy, every Italian Democratic leader in the State of New York has been purged, including Carmine DeSapio, the former Tammany Hall leader and National Committeeman in New York State.

I am the only Democratic leader in the State of New York who has survived the purge.

For the past 3 years since Bobby Kennedy became Senator of New York, several attempted purges have been made on me.

I was successful in fighting off the first purge led by Tom Gilroy and only a year ago by Paul Mullen, who fought the organization attempting to wrest control of the Democratic party from the present leadership.

And now in a third attempt, Mr. Kennedy comes to Utica to back a lifelong Republican, who two years ago ran in the Republican Primary against Mayor Frank Dulan, then as a Liberal Party candidate and at present as a Democratic candidate to break the strength of the East Utica Democratic Organization hoping to turn the Democratic Party in Oneida County over to Bobby Kennedy.

If during my years of leadership of the East Utica Democratic organization I have in any small way been responsible for doing you or your family a favor, I am now asking you personally to save the strength of the Democratic Party in East Utica by casting your vote for Sebastian M. Convertino for Mayor, a life-long Democrat.

SAL by unanimous decision was nominated for Mayor by the City Executive Committee and the full City Committee because he was the best qualified candidate and I still feel the same way.

However, if Mr. Assaro is elected Mayor, we are virtually turning the Democratic Party over to Mr. Kennedy and Mr. Burns.

Sincerely,

Rufus P. Elefante

RUFUS P. ELEFANTE

P.S. Convertino's ballot number is 14-D — Row D.

LONG-HAIRED DECISION—Senator Kennedy, during his visit to Utica late last month, when he said he "wouldn't cut his hair until Dick Assaro was elected mayor."

★ ★ ★ ★ ★ ★

Assaro Victory Spells Doom for Old Machine

By ED BYRNE

The big question following each of the past four mayoral elections has been the fate of long-time East Utica Democratic political boss Rufus P. Elefante.

There has been no real answer until yesterday when neo-Democrat Dominick Assaro dumped four-term Republican Mayor Frank M. Dulan.

It now appears extremely unlikely that the old guard Democratic organization led by Elefante and centered in East Utica, has any shred of hope for a comeback.

• • •

ASSARO NOT ONLY WON the mayoralty, he became the city's top Democrat and the city's top Italian Democrat, positions that have been held by Elefante for years.

The probability is that movements will be started to oust both City Democratic Chairman Alfred Mirante and Oneida County Chairman G. Carl Morse.

Going into the election Assaro did not have near the committeemen's votes to dump either man. However, this is expected to change markedly when committee members start reviewing on which side their bread is buttered.

• • •

ASSARO WOULD NOT COMMENT today on the possibility that his group would act to take over the organization that he beat in the June 21 primary.

Morse forecast a switch of allegiance with the Assaro win, but said it hadn't given him any thoughts of resigning.

"The problem," he said, "is not a problem of who's going to be boss politically. From the exhibition yesterday, if the Democratic Party wants to survive, they had all better participate. That's been their trouble — too many bosses and not enough workers."

Mirante could not be reached.

The 1970s

In the spring of 1972, Marino's Restaurant, for many decades the nerve center of Elefante's political machine, fell victim to Urban Renewal. However, even though Marino's final days understandably inspired nostalgia, Elefante barely missed a beat, as he soon established a new headquarters at Uncle Henry's Pancake House in an effort to keep his battered but still viable political organization in operation. Indeed, by the time Marino's had fallen to the wrecking ball, Elefante had already set into motion a series of tactical maneuvers that would give his political career a new lease on life. Having been blocked repeatedly in his attempts to regain influence at City Hall by backing Democrats for Mayor, Elefante threw his support behind a Republican, local businessman Mike Caruso, who defeated Assaro in 1971.

The mayoral election of 1973 witnessed a three-way race between Caruso, Democratic nominee and Elefante loyalist Sal Convertino, and Edward A. Hanna, a one-time Elefante protégé who spent much of his career in what one might characterize as a political "love-hate" relationship with the aging East Utica leader. Hanna ran in 1973 on an "anti-Rufie" platform, but after his election, in a typically unpredictable turnaround, he offered Elefante an unpaid position as "Advisor to the Mayor" and proclaimed April 7, 1974, to be "Rufus P. Elefante Day." However, in little more than six months, the two men had parted ways, as Elefante resigned from his advisory post ostensibly to tend to personal business. The mercurial Hanna returned to his anti-Rufie line and was elected, again as an independent, to a second term in 1975.

While he certainly had his hardcore supporters, Hanna also made many enemies, and in so doing, he created an opening for Elefante to stage an indisputable comeback as the single-most important local Democratic leader. In 1977, longtime Elefante loyalist Steve Pawlinga, who had a significant following in predominantly Polish West Utica, defeated Hanna with Elefante's support. In 1979, Elefante and his allies helped Pawlinga to gain re-election as an independent after the Mayor lost the Democratic primary to Louis LaPolla. Pawlinga's dramatic come-from-behind victory seemed to confirm that Rufie had regained his old political magic.

Elefante's political renewal was noted by politicians well beyond the boundaries of Oneida County. Governor Hugh Carey periodically gave Elefante a respectful nod and a favor, and the Carter administration tossed Utica Urban Renewal grants. Among other things, the Pawlinga administration used federal largesse to build a hotel complex on the former site of Utica's old City Hall; the parcel had been cleared in 1968 in preparation for an Urban Renewal project only to languish for a decade, an unsightly mud hole on Utica's main street that had become an embarrassment to the community. By the end of the 1970s, it therefore seemed that the old Elefante machine, though much diminished by the political struggles of the late 1950s and the 1960s, was itself experiencing renewal. Although his moment of triumph was to be shorter-lived than even his critics might at that point have imagined, few figures arguably would have survived politically so long as had Elefante, particularly after such sustained efforts to end his influence.

1970s

Rufie and grandson Dr. Rufus P. Collea

From Rufie, A Toast to Yesterday

For 'Little City Hall', Look Back in Sadness

By ED BYRNE

The wreckers will come Thursday or Friday to knock it down. They will knock it down because it is needed for development of Parcel 7 in the John Bleecker Urban Renewal Project.

There will be no footnotes. If it is not unattractive, the simple frame structure is neither big enough nor grandiose enough to qualify for scenic or historic preservation.

Yet, within its shadow grey-green confines, more history was made than in any building in Utica.

Marino's Restaurant was Democratic headquarters for more than a half century. It was where the action was, where the Old Man, Rufie Elefante and his predecessors at the Democratic helm held forth.

• • •

RUFIE WAS AT the farewell party last week, with many of Marino's other regulars. Some were missing, having bid their final farewells earlier. People like Lt. Gov. Bill Bray, or Charlie Donnelly, or Frank Marino, one of the two brothers that ran the restaurant for years. Frank died in December.

The young folks wouldn't remember them. Nor would they remember U.S. Senator James Mead, who Rufie says, "was Utica's godfather."

Rufie recalls when "Jim Mead and Charlie Donnelly and myself sat down in Marinos when they were going to put an Air Force base at Dunkirk.

"Dunkirk was flat," Rufie recalls, "and that's why they were going to put the air base there. But Jim Mead had the Army engineers look for a site around here and that is how Griffiss Air Force Base (at Rome) came to be."

That was the kind of decision that was made at Marino's. It was a regular stop for the city's Democratic mayors, for its judges—people like federal judge Steve Brennan, county judge Ezra Hannigan or city judge John T. Buckley, all having passed on. Or for people like former State Democratic Chairman Dick Balch.

When they came to town, people like Lt. Gov. Charles Polletti, or Senator Wagner, or his son, former New York City Mayor Bob Wagner, dropped in.

So did some non-political types, like Joe DiMaggio or Jimmy Durante.

• • •

THEY CALLED IT Litttle City Hall, the restaurant at Catherine and First Streets. And this week it will come down, as a result of a decision made by an administration foreign to its occupants in the early 1960s.

It was a tavern over the last 90 years, known earlier as Manzi's and Girard's, and then 60 years ago, as Marino's, when Joe and Frank's father, Emilio, ran it.

Joe and Frank Marino bought the land back from urban renewal and took out a building permit in December for a new restaurant. Joe has been close-mouthed about his intentions.

• • •

IN THE MEANTIME, much of the old line Democrats' political conversation, if not all of their policy making, has

(Continued on Page 3B)

RUFIE'S BOOTH — A serious moment, mirroring many such moments of the past, when Rufie expounded and others listened, which frequently didn't require the best ears in town. From left, Tommy Ruggiero, Rufie, Jake Goldbas, Muzzy Tomaino.

THE OFFCE — This is Marino's "office," — more of a small conference room — where many of tne city's major decisions were made. From left, Rufie, Muzzy Tomaino, Joe Marino, Tony Cortese, Tommy Ruggiero. (Photos by James Armstrong).

Louis STEPPELLO

JOE

Louie Steppello, Bob DiBrango, Rufie, Mayor Pawlinga, Carmen Pacicca, and Joe Marino

Mr. Elefante Still The Politician

Rufus P. Elefante had a little difficulty Thursday living up to his new image as Utica's elder statesman. Events of the day—centering around Mayor Hanna's surprise, unqualified endorsement of Republican Governor Malcolm Wilson—proved that Rufie is still very much a political man.

Rufie was the unchallenged, Democratic overlord in these parts for years. One story should suffice to suggest the scope of his former power: when the late Robert F. Kennedy came to town several years ago, and was being driven to a downtown affair, the car passed Mr. Elefante's house.

"Say, isn't that where Rufie lives?" asked Kennedy.

Mr. Elefante had dropped further out of the limelight, which he always shunned, in recent years. Rufie is retired, they said. Sure, he tried like heck to have Sebastian Convertino, the Democrat, beat Edward Hanna, the independent Democrat, last year—Convertino long was Rufie's fair-haired boy, and besides, Hanna and Elefante didn't much like each other anymore—but this was nothing more than the old Democratic kingpin turning his life-long avocation into a retirement hobby.

Then, the surprise. Hanna, after stunning Convertino and Republican Mayor Caruso, offered Rufie a job in City Hall as the mayor's unsalaried adviser. Rufie, reportedly no longer eager to wield political power, but captivated with the thought of becoming an elder statesman who could advise the city along favorable paths, accepted the mayor's offer.

Mr. Elefante has denied that the old bug of political power still whispers in his ear—that those whispers have been manifested in the hiring of Corporation Counsel Stephen Pawlinga, City Planner Samuel Russo, and pressures on personnel at the auditorium and on the police force. There was nothing you could put your finger on substantially to say that Rufie was back politically.

Rufie left no doubts about that Thursday. He was so incensed when he learned that Hanna was going to endorse Wilson, that he shunned the mayor and Mrs. Wilson. According to Elefante, Pawlinga and former Corporation Counsel Joe Scarfarotti joined him to make it three sets of cold shoulders.

The city's former Democratic kingpin shed his statesmanship quick enough in turning his back on the state's first lady. But he couldn't contain himself. He took the opportunity to express his displeasure at former Democratic Mayor Dominick Assaro, an arch-enemy of Elefante, who happens to be running the area campaign of Representative Hugh Carey, Wilson's Democratic opponent.

"I think Carey has to make a choice as to who he will follow: Assaro or County (Democratic) Chairman Ray Stefano," Mr. Elefante said. That sounds like the Rufie of yesteryear, enamored of the political arena, and active therein.

Mr. Hanna clearly has a right to endorse anyone he wishes for governor, but he just may have lost a sometimes statesman in the bargain. It might not be visible right away, but wait until the mayoral election next year.

Old Foes Meet in City Hall

Hanna Says Today's 'Rufus P. Elefante Day'

By ED RUFFING

"If I was a lot younger, I'd take a job with you (Mayor Hanna) to get this city moving in the right direction — and, I'd do it for 50 cents a year salary," Rufus P. Elefante, the legendary Democratic leader, said yesterday in an hour long visit to City Hall.

Elefante came to the meeting with ideas and left with a proclamation designating today as Rufus P. Elefante Day in Utica. "The first one I ever received," Rufie said.

Elefante, making his first "official" visit to a mayor's office in the city accepted an invitation to "talk things over to get Utica moving" with Mayor Edward A. Hanna.

It was a "mutual admiration society" meeting as the two opposites forgot poltic and concentrated on what could be done t attract industry such as the Mille Brewing Co.

Photo by George Widman

Mayor Hanna and Rufus P. Elefante

RUFUS P. ELEFANTE
ADVISOR TO THE MAYOR

1 Kennedy Plaza
Utica, New York 13502

Phone 315 / 798-3200

THE CITY OF UTICA

EDWARD A. HANNA, MAYOR

CITY HALL — UTICA, NEW YORK 13502

Proclamation

RUFUS P. ELEFANTE DAY

Sunday, April 7, 1974

Whereas, Rufus P. Elefante has honored City Hall by visiting with the Mayor personally today to offer advice, suggestions and help pertaining to the improvement of good government and the betterment of city life for all citizens and,

Whereas, Mr. Rufus P. Elefante has demonstrated a desire to offer, on a voluntary basis, any help that he is able to give and especially,

Whereas, The meeting demonstrated a fine atmosphere, with no discussion, whatsoever, relating to politics, and,

Whereas, We expect to take advantage of Rufus P. Elefante's good counsel and experience and gain by it. (We might even get him to contribute a few bucks.) and,

Whereas, It is time we started honoring this gentlemen for the many good things he as done for the community,

Therefofe, I, Edward A. Hanna, Mayor of the City of Utica, State of New York do hereby proclaim Sunday, April 7, 1974 as:

RUFUS P. ELEFANTE DAY

April 7, 1974
Date

Edward A. Hanna
Edward A. Hanna, Mayor

After 7 Months

Elefante Resigns City Hall Post

By DENNEY CLEMENTS

After seven months as Mayor Hanna's unpaid adviser, Rufus P. Elefante today tendered his resignation to the mayor.

In his letter of resignation, Elefante cited "the present business recession" as his reason for leaving, adding: "I must devote my entire time to my financial interests."

Hanna, asked for comment on the resignation, said: "What the hell are you bothering me for? I've got work to do here today."

He also said the Utica newspapers had lost their "credibility" with him.

The mayor would not comment directly on Elefante's resignation.

Elefante, who was contacted by a reporter in Uncle Henry's Pancake House late this morning, would make no further comment or elaborate on the letter.

o o o

WITH ELEFANTE at Uncle Henry's was Corporation Counsel Stephen Pawlinga, who also made no comment when asked if he, too, had resigned or planned to resign. He said he is still corporation counsel.

Speculation that Pawlinga and Elefante would resign reached its peak yesterday. A number of sources reported that the resignations were imminent. Both men remained silent on those reports yesterday.

Earlier this morning, in Hanna's office, Pawlinga was asked directly by the mayor if he had written a resignation letter, and replied, in a reporter's presence: "I haven't drawn up any letter."

Pawlinga has been an Elefante polictical and legal associate more than 15 years.

o o o

IN HIS LETTER to the mayor, Elefante said, "I want to thank you for the opportunity you gave me in trying to help Utica.

"I also want to thank you for the very nice things you have done for me and said about me publicly.

"Due to the present business recession, I find that I must devote my entire time to my financial interests.

"I feel confident that you are on your way and will succeed in your endeavors to get downtown moving for our city.

RUFUS ELEFANTE

"Let me thank you again for the opportunity of serving in your administration."

o o o

ELEFANTE went to work for Hanna in April, saying that the mayor had offered him "a place in the sun."

The linking of Hanna with Elefante surprised many Uticans as the two had split publicly after Hanna won election to the state Assembly in 1965. From that time on, the two were said to be political enemies.

Elefante kept a low public profile while a mayoral aide, most often surfacing to participate in Hanna's efforts to stimulate redevelopment in the two blocks bounded by Genesee,

(Continued on Page 7)

We Need a 'Boss'

By Hyman Sternberg
Higby Rd., New Hartford

An article in the July 10 issue of Newsweek magazine, entitled "Shake the Money Tree," points out how most urban problems seem to be getting worse despite billions spent by the federal government. The article, however, cites Peekskill, New York, as one example of a dying city revived and rejuvenated by good planning, good organization and a community effort by local merchants and other citizens. The method used in Peekskill was simply to hire a "boss" for the hob.

What about Utica?

The "boss" has been characterized as the beast of American politics but where has Utica gone without the guiding hand of the old fashioned politician who had the strength and the guts to mold a political organization into a unified force; a force that could and did get things done for Utica without a lot of namby-pamby shining, theoretical concepts, abstract promises and general do-nothingism.

Utica is plagued by a modern disease, the young man in politics who rides into office with his fancy diploma, high salary and high sounding philosophy. He is more concerned with making headlines than finishing a job. He devastates an urban renewal project and leaves half of a downtown demolished. He gives away prime tax paying property. He drives half of the downtown merchants to the suburbs and expects the remaining merchants to make up the tax loss. He patronizes the shopping centers by sending buses to the outlying districts, but he ignores the ever increasing parking problem in the city itself. Finally, he promises that by 1985 the inner city will be rebuilt. In truth, by 1985, he will have destroyed the downtown merchants and the inner city will be a desolate waste.

When the term "boss" is mentioned in Utica, certain names come to mind. The city has not been kind to these names. Yet, these men accomplished things; they had the good of the city at heart, for they, like your writer, were born and raised here. The city was good to them and they were good to it. But the good that has been done is oft forgotten while the endless name-calling continues. At every election the hue and cry goes out "we are clean politicians, we have no connection with the 'boss'." As a simple matter of fact, the new politicians can name call, but they cannot get a job done. They want to be bosses themselves once elected but they simply lack the necessary experience.

Utica needs help. It is time for politicians to stop bickering for the sake of headlines and to start supporting their city. We cannot wait until 1885 to see results. A concerted effort in Peekskill behind a city "boss" saved the city. In Peekskill, a "boss" had to be brought in for the job. Utica has its own "elder statesmen" often called "bosses" on the scene, ready for the job. They did the job in the past and they can do it again. A fund established by the business people of the community would get them started. They need only to be called.

—Community Forum—

Machine Politics Defended

By J. Richard Emmert

4 Humphrey Terrace, New Hartford

Your recent editorial on machine politics was somewhat shallow. Contrary to your assertion that "a politcal scientist could not have described the operation of a machine better," the fact is that few political scientists would explain the significance of political machines (or party organizations) solely, or even primarily, in terms of removing trees, cleaning up leaves or finding jobs.

Doing favors (and expecting them to be repaid) is, of course, one of the more apparent activities of political bosses (or party leaders) but a more careful examination of the reasons why this occurs would have led to a less superficial conclusion.

Inadvertently you suggest (but do not pursue) the answer when you describe Rufus Elefante as "the mechanic who kept the machine running...(with his)..."wheeling and dealing." As a mechanic (or broker or coalition-builder), Mr. Elefante has been relatively effective over the years in winning elections for his candidates but, as any political scientist would have told you, that is understandable.

The primary task of a political boss (or party leader) has always been to piece together the disparate groups which exist in any community until he has the majority that enables his machine (or political party) to win public office.

Perhaps if you had dwelt more on this essestial task of party leaders and political organizations, and less on superficial but more apparent activities, you would not have drawn the unwarranted conclusion that political machines (or party organizations) are an affront to democracy.

What is so undemocratic about building coalitions and constructing majorities? Is that not necessary if those who win power are to govern in the interests of as many citizens as possible?

If you had consulted a political scientist, chances are that you would have been told that, if democracy is to be sustained, it is not only good but essential that someone performs this task.

In terms of this larger task, then, the question of whose trees are removed or whose leaves are picked up (however annoying and petty such behavior might be) fades into insignificance.

In the future it might be a good idea to consult several political scientists before you evoke their expertise in defense of your conclusions. And, in all fairness, if you think some of the foregoing points have merit, should you not write a new editorial with the following headline: Observer Dispatch Editorial Wins Recognition But Lacks Credibility.

Steve Pawlinga, Rufie, Sue Baum, John Ventura, Governor Hugh Carey

You are cordially invited to attend the Inauguration

of

Hugh L. Carey

as Governor of the State of New York

in the Assembly Chamber of the State Capitol at Albany

January first, nineteen hundred and seventy-nine

at twelve-thirty o'clock

Rufie and Mayor Steve Pawlinga

The beginning of the decade witnessed the closure of Uncle Henry's Pancake House. Elefante therefore opened what would be his final, semi-official headquarters, the Franklin D. Roosevelt Democratic Club, in a storefront on Bleecker Street. He also held court with friends and allies over lunch at the Alpine East Restaurant on Albany Street. Elefante also held court daily over lunch at the Alpine East Restaurant on Albany Street.

Old allegations that the Democrats had been too lenient toward unsavory elements in Utica continued to surface periodically into the 1980s, much to Elefante's irritation and that of his allies, and he continued to respond to such allegations as aggressively as ever. In 1982, the host of a local radio talk show failed to challenge a caller who stated, in reference to Elefante, that "we all know he's a Mafia boss." A swift threat of legal action resulted in a public apology from the station, but the whole incident only served to reanimate resentments among at least some local Italian Americans, who felt that East Utica and Rufie Elefante had long been victims of ethnic stereotyping and scandal-mongering. Indeed, critics of Elefante often seemed to be unaware or uninterested in the fact that the machine had always thrived to some extent on Italian American memories of the prejudice they and their relatives had endured—that criticism of Rufie, historically one of the leading figures in the local Italian ethnic community, only tended to strengthen his standing among Italian American voters for much of his career.

The electoral victories Elefante and Pawlinga had enjoyed in the late 1970s, along with the patronage they received from the Carter administration and the political friendliness of Governor Carey, seemed to presage a renewal of the machine's powers. However, at this crucial juncture, when he was seemingly in the midst of a remarkable late-in-life comeback, Elefante and his local allies made a significant, if understandable, political miscalculation. In 1982, Hugh Carey announced he was stepping down as Governor. New York City Mayor Ed Koch quickly emerged as the leading contender for the Democratic nomination to be Carey's successor, although he was challenged by Lieutenant Governor Mario Cuomo, who was widely characterized as the underdog. Koch was the "smart" choice: he had begun to turn around New York City, which had lapsed into seemingly endless chaos and decline since the mid-1960s, and his candor appealed to many people, even in upstate New York—when it comes to frankness, upstaters are not so different from downstaters as historical regional antipathies might suggest. Nevertheless, there is just so much candor upstate voters can tolerate, particularly when it emanates from The City.

Elefante, like most of the state party establishment, lined up behind Koch when the New York City Mayor's fortunes were riding high. For his part, Koch paid homage to the East Utica leader by visiting Elefante at his home during a campaign stop in Utica. However, Koch's candidacy began to implode when he gave an interview to *Playboy* magazine in which he unwisely suggested he had scant regard for upstate New York. At the same time, many Italian Americans increasingly responded to the prospect of an Italian American Governor. In the 1982 Democratic primaries, Mario Cuomo therefore swept all but one of Utica's wards, including all of East Utica, notwithstanding a brave effort by Elefante's allies to contain the damage Koch had inflicted on himself and his local supporters.

With Cuomo's victory, Elefante began slowly and quietly to withdraw from politics. However, the period had its compensations. Hugh Carey had appointed Elefante to the New York State Franklin Delano Roosevelt Centennial Commission, a body that included such luminaries as Lauren Bacall, Walter Cronkite, Averell Harriman, Margaret Truman, Franklin Roosevelt, Jr., Robert F. Wagner, Theodore H. White, David Rockefeller, and Cyrus Vance. Although the appointment was largely honorary, it gave Elefante an opportunity to enjoy recognition of the fact that he and similar local political leaders—the now largely disappeared urban ethnic political bosses—had collectively played an important role in the electoral victories of Franklin Roosevelt and the triumph of the New Deal.

Elefante's last great crusade was to protect what he considered the best interests of the Utica Board of Water Supply. The Board was created when a private concern, the Utica Water Company, was purchased by the City of Utica in the 1930s with the help of a federally-subsidized loan arranged through the East Utica machine's connections in Washington. In 1986 Elefante published an editorial, in his capacity as a member of the water board, in which he noted that his old nemesis, Governor Dewey, had approved legislation that had permitted suburban communities to tax water board assets located within their boundaries. Such legislation, he forcefully argued, had undermined the ability of the water board to modernize just as some of those very suburban communities had begun to experience dramatic growth that placed increasing demands on the water system. Utica taxpayers, he argued, had therefore footed some part of the cost that facilitated suburban growth.

This history lesson—as some of the newspaper's editors had initially tried to dismiss his editorial—and Elefante's plea for fairness to Utica was particularly significant because John H. McMillan, publisher of the *Observer-Dispatch*, wrote a companion piece to it in which he generally supported Elefante's position, saying baldly that "the nation's cities, including Utica, have been exploited." In addition, McMillan asserted that First Amendment protections belong "to all the people...not just to companies that own the printing presses," thus essentially conceding some part of Elefante's long-time contention that he had been compelled for decades to battle the accusations of a powerful national newspaper chain in an era in which newspapers had been at the peak of their power to shape public opinion.

For his part, Elefante seems to have been genuinely grateful to McMillan, and the long-standing feud between Elefante and the local newspapers, which had been slowly cooling for at least a decade, pretty much came to an end. Periodically throughout the remainder of his life, the *Observer-Dispatch* published pieces which, if they did not entirely validate Elefante's perspective on his life story, were nevertheless more sympathetic and even somewhat nostalgic about the East Utica leader's career.

Scholars and publications outside the Utica area also began to recognize in Elefante a survivor of another era—of a time, by then a half-century away, when urban political bosses and the powerful, patronage-driven organizations they led, had helped to build majorities for the Democratic Party, supported the New Deal, and thus saved many from hardship during the Great Depression. In 1990, when Bernie Sanders—later a United States Senator from Vermont, but at that time a visiting faculty member at nearby Hamilton College—wrote to Elefante to ask if he might interview him, Sanders observed: "the role that you have played in Utica politics and city government is well known throughout the country by those of us interested in local politics."

In 1989, the *New York Times* mentioned Elefante in the same breath as Chicago's legendary, and controversial, Mayor Richard Daley, saying that Elefante had once run a city in which "patronage jobs were handed out from restaurant booths," and it observed that urban leaders of such power as Daley and Elefante had disappeared "along with the old working-class ethnic neighborhoods," like lower East Utica, that had once served as their bases of power. In writing to Elefante's daughter the same year to ask if he might interview Rufie, the political journalist Alan Ehrenhalt stated: "the fact is, Rufus Elefante is an important figure in 20th century urban history, and his views are important for posterity." Ehrenhalt incorporated his interview with Elefante into an article on Utica, published in *Governing* magazine, that subsequently provided the basis for a chapter in Ehrenhalt's respected 1991 book on American politics, *The United States of Ambition.*

The *Observer-Dispatch* serialized Ehrenhalt's chapter on Elefante, and Uticans avidly read and debated the piece. The series elicited a characteristically satirical response from the newspaper's popular editorial cartoonist, Randall Kimberley, and representatives of some Italian American organizations objected to references in it to the Sin City scandal. Nevertheless, two-thirds of Uticans polled in this period by the *Observer-Dispatch* indicated they thought Utica would be better off if the city still had an old-style political machine such as Elefante had run.

In a May 1992 interview with the *Observer-Dispatch*, the 89 year-old Elefante admitted that he had essentially retired from politics, although he still maintained contacts with political figures both inside and beyond Utica, including two Republicans of note, Senator Alphonse D'Amato and Utica's Congressman Sherwood Boehlert, who would become a leading figure among moderate Republicans in the House of Representatives in the mid-1990s. The newspaper noted in 1992 that, despite "aches and pains, Rufie looks remarkably fit," and in fact he remained extremely active until quite late in life. However, in second half of 1994, his health began to decline dramatically, requiring several months of hospitalization that ended with his death on November 15 at the age of 91.

Long-time critics and devoted followers—as well as the many whose views fell somewhere in between—came forward to acknowledge Elefante's political skills and to hail him as the last of a breed. Nationally-noted local pollster John Zogby fittingly observed that the decline of the strong party loyalties that had prevailed in Elefante's heyday and the rise of television as a key factor in national political life had made it unlikely there would ever be another figure of his kind. Elefante and his allies were not just local political power brokers—they belonged to networks of similar figures and local organizations throughout the country that collectively influenced the choice of candidates for national, as well as state and local, office. At the risk of seeming to romanticize, the ability of the machines like Elefante's to exercise such influence depended not so much on trickery or simply on the distribution of patronage, but on unsung neighborhood party workers who cultivated voters at the street-level, heard their complaints and concerns, and worked hard to bring them into the political process—albeit, to bring them into the process as loyal clients of the organization.

Today's elected officials are no longer beholden to party "bosses," and candidates can now supposedly speak directly to the voters without the approval of party leaders or access to the organizational resources of urban political machines. However, today's candidates—particularly those for state and national office—speak very frequently by way of expensive 30-second television commercials that are bankrolled by unelected moneyed interests that typically seek to oversimplify public debate and often do not have the ties to average people at the grassroots level such as the old-time urban machines possessed. In addition, the so-called "24-hour news cycle," which requires an endless flow of material, regardless of whether it is newsworthy or adequately considered by those who present it, has also increased the role of television in shaping—and distorting—political discourse in this country. One does not need to be a fan of political machines or bosses to wonder whether the elimination of such organizations, and the general weakening of party loyalties, has really made civic life any more virtuous, efficient, or responsive to average people than typified government before the rise of television. One might very well argue that the contrary is the case, and yet without reinventing old-time political machines—an unlikely event that few would admit they would like to see—the only alternative is for individual citizens to shoulder more responsibility by becoming both deeply and broadly informed, stronger advocates for themselves, and maintaining active engagement with the political process even when that process seems alienating, confusing, and inconveniently time-consuming. In the absence of the widespread commitment to an enhanced sense civic responsibility, in the age in which we live, no organization or political leader can or arguably will succeed in promoting the public interest.

Observer-Dispatch file photo

After Marino's Restaurant was torn down in 1972, Uncle Henry's Pancake House, shown here in a 1981 photo, became Rufus Elefante's political headquarters.

Another 'Little City Hall' Might Soon Be Only History

O-D Photo by Mike Doherty

By TIM RICE

Most of its patrons say it never quite made the grade as a successor to Marino's Restaurant, once known as Utica's "Little City Hall."

It didn't have the charm, they say. It was too public. No place could ever match Marino's for food, drink and political backroom atmosphere.

But for the past ten years, Uncle Henry's Pancake House on LaFayette Street has filled an important void in Utica by playing host to the area's top politicians and Democratic Party officials.

On Nov. 30 that role will apparently end: Uncle Henry's is to go on the block at a foreclosure sale.

THE RESTAURANT'S OWNER, Henry Cittadino, declined to discuss the foreclosure, but he has been trying to sell the restaurant for a year and is reportedly in poor health. According to court papers filed by Marine Midland Bank, Cittadino owes nearly $31,000 in mortgage payments and $14,000 in unpaid federal taxes.

"Yes, I think this is the end of an era," says Rufus P. Elefante, Utica's long-time Democratic kingpin. "I hope someone buys it. It's been a good spot."

Since Marino's closed in 1972, "Rufie" has held court daily in Henry's, and has become its most famous patron. Don't bother calling his home, insiders say. If you have business with Elefante, leave word at Henry's.

ELEFANTE and Cittadino, who is better known as "Uncle Henry," are long-time friends, but Elefante said he has no plans to buy the restaurant. "I don't know anything about buying it," he says. "I've been too busy with the campaign to think about it."

Franklin D. Roosevelt
DEMOCRATIC CLUB
F.D.R.
DEMOCRATIC
CLUB
"TOGETHER WE CANNOT FAIL"
MEMBERS
WELCOME
DEMOCRATIC
CLUB

New Headquarters Is Bleecker St. Site, Elefante Declares

Utica O-D
Tue 1/5/1982 p 9

By DAVID E. WILLIAMS

ELEFANTE

Rufus Elefante, old-guard East Utica Democratic leader, said today that since Uncle Henry's Pancake House closed, he's been spreading his business around at "a couple of dozen restaurants."

For years the pancake house was a popular meeting place for area politicians, and it was often said to be Elefante's unofficial headquarters. However, owner Henry Cittadino closed the restaurant last month after Marine Midland Bank, holder of a $31,000 mortgage, was the only bidder at a foreclosure sale.

When he's not at a restaurant, Elefante said, he can often be found at the party's new "official" headquarters, at 232 Bleecker St.

There's no food service at the new headquarters, just a coffee pot, but its still "a place you can run politics from," Elefante said. He said the Democrats moved in last May, and the decision to open a headquarters had nothing to do with the closing of Uncle Henry's.

Elefante said the headquarters included two connecting store fronts and a rear office. He said the Democratic City Committee rented it from Paul Paladino for $200 a month, and the committee must pay for all utilities.

Elefante said party and city officials and party committeemen frequent the headquarters, some visiting daily, and it is a place to hold meetings.

He said a permanent headquarters was "long overdue," and he said the Republicans had a permanent headquarters on Steuben Park. The Democrats last had a permanent headquarters about five years ago, in a suite at the Hotel Utica, Elefante said.

Elefante Suing Radio Station

OD July 31, 1982

Charging that his reputation has been defamed, East Utica Democratic leader Rufus P. Elefante has filed a $2.6 million suit against radio station WTLB, which he says aired remarks by a caller who referred to him as a Mafia boss on March 11.

Elefante contends that station employees were negligent in failing to use a seven-second delay mechanism to prevent the remark from being aired.

Art Levy, the host of "WTLB Live," is accused of being malicious and disregarding the truth by encouraging the caller to continue talking about Elefante's "alleged connection with the Mafia." The suit contends that Levy knew the statement was false or he failed to take the proper steps to determine whether the statement was true or false.

In a complaint filed by attorney Antonio Faga, who is Elefante's newphew, Elfante said he has "enjoyed a good reputation for honesty, uprightness of character and a complete non-affiliation with the organization known as the Mafia."

Elefante also contends that WTLB President Paul Dunn was negligent in making a transcript of the conversation between Levy and the caller available to a variety of people in a "grossly irresponsible manner."

According to the transcript, the caller told Levy:

"OK. That gentleman that just called, he wanted to know about Rufus Elefante, you know. OK. Well, he's supposed to be a ... well ... we all know he's a Mafia boss ... you know ... for the city."

The caller also said that everyone in East Utica knew about Elefante's connection with the Mafia and that his position as a Utica Board of Water Supply commissioner was "only a front."

Dunn, Levy and WTLB vice president Edward J. Carey could not be reached for comment.

The station's lawyers have 20 days to answer the complaint.

Elefante gets apology from radio station

By KEN SCHAAF
For The Daily Press

Daily Press Thur May 19, 1983

A $2.6 million lawsuit brought by Democratic leader Rufus Elefante against a local radio station charging slander was settled for an apology contained in a full-page advertisement in yesterday's Utica newspapers.

The written apology to Elefante was made by Paul Dunn, president of WTLB radio. The only money involved in the settlement was for Elefante's legal services during the suit. Attorney Antonio Faga, Elefante's nephew, said his uncle was pleased with the apology. Faga declined to say what his legal fee would be.

Elefante couldn't be reached for comment at Democratic headquarters on Bleecker Street.

Dunn said he wrote the apology, which included a paragraph in which he praised Elefante for donating his "fine efforts and good judgment for the betterment of our community." That paragraph was requested by Elefante and added by Dunn himself, he said.

The advertisement, which appeared in the Daily Press and Observer-Dispatch, cost about $2,000, Dunn said.

Dunn said he thought the settlement was fair. He declined further comment.

Elefante's suit said a caller to WTLB Live, an afternoon talk show, made an erroneous allegation about Elefante's "alleged connection with the Mafia." The suit also said the caller erroneously claimed Elefante's job as a Utica Board of Water Supply commissioner was only a front.

Elefante contended in the papers that the radio station could have used delay equipment it had installed to stop the remarks from being aired. He also contended that Art Levy, the show's host, knew the statement was false or that he failed to take proper steps to determine whether the statement was true or false before allowing it on the air.

Mayor Steve Pawlinga, Rufie and Mayor Ed Koch

* The Daily Press, Monday, April 19, 1982/3

Koch meets with Rufie

By MARTY TYKSINSKI
For The Daily Press

New York City Mayor Edward Koch delayed a cocktail party appearance before about 100 area Democrats at the Sheraton Hotel last night to meet privately with Rufus P. Elefante at the home of the Democratic leader.

Koch said the purpose of the private meeting was to court Elefante's support in his bid for the Democratic nomination for governor. He would not discuss the details of their conversation.

When asked if Elefante agreed to back his candidacy, Koch answered, "I'm not going to get into that." Koch called Elefante "one of the most influential political leaders in the area."

Koch was scheduled to hold a press conference at 7:45 and to make an appearance at the cocktail party at 8, but he did not arrive until after 9.

Martin McLaughlin, Koch's press secretary, said the meeting was a surprise, both to Koch and Elefante. "I don't think it was planned because Rufie was shocked," he said.

McLaughlin said the meeting included Koch, Elefante, Mayor Stephen Pawlinga and "a couple of other people," but said he did not know who the others were. He said the meeting lasted about 20 minutes.

Pawlinga, who sported a "Koch for Governor" button on his lapel, had no comment on the private meeting or whether he is endorsing Koch for governor. "I will make an appropriate announcement at an appropriate time," he said.

Pawlinga said the absence of Oneida County Democratic Chairwoman Mary Lou Bartlett was not "a snub" against Koch. He said Bartlett co-signed the invitations but did not come because she was bowling in a championship tournament.

Koch and 'Rufie': Dubious Meeting

On his recent visit to Utica, New York City Mayor Ed Koch kept about 100 potential supporters cooling their heels at a cocktail party while he paid homage to local Democratic kingpin Rufus Elefante.

Koch, who is running for governor, obviously hoped to ingratiate himself to the longtime political power broker. But it makes you wonder what his honor's priorities are, and more importantly, how he will perceive his duties if he is elected.

It was bad enough that Koch felt he had to see "the boss." It was worse when he made his followers wait at the well while he went in alone to kneel at the shrine.

Yes, Ed, we know the explanation. As a politician, you've got to do these things to get elected. It doesn't mean you will be obligated to Elefante if he helps you in the trenches on election day.

Sure.

It's ironic. Because Koch likes to portray himself as the people's mayor. No doubt he will be advertising himself as the people's candidate for governor, too. Come to think of it, he never did say which people.

Elefante is a political force in this city for one reason. He has amassed thousands of "political IOUs" over the years by doling out favors. He did it, not as an elected official accountable to the voters, but as a puppeteer pulling strings.

Sometimes Elefante's machinations have benefited Utica. Often times they have not. But always, the top priority has been — and is — to hold political power.

EDWARD I. KOCH

April 28, 1982

Dear Rufie:

It was really a pleasure to meet you. I do hope that we can be on a first-name basis.

I am very grateful for your support and for your having so forthrightly told me that you will help in getting a large vote for me in Utica. I am committed, if given the chance, to being a governor who will serve all of the people of this state in the tradition of our great democratic governors -- Al Smith, Franklin Roosevelt, Herbert Lehman, Averill Harriman and Hugh Carey.

I look forward to our working together not only during the primary and the general election but in the years to come should I be elected.

All the best.

Sincerely,

Ed

Edward I. Koch
Mayor

Mr. Rufus Elefante
232 Bleecker Street
Utica, New York 13501

Elefante Named to Panel To Plan FDR Centennial

By TIM RICE

More than 50 years ago, at the age of 28, a young Rufus P. Elefante gathered nearly 10,000 Uticans at Mohawk and Bleecker streets to greet the Democratic candidate for governor, Franklin Delano Roosevelt.

Roosevelt's 1928 campaign had begun a week earlier with stops in Buffalo, Rochester and Syracuse. They were all flops. Then he hit Utica.

"FDR was elated at the turnout. He said it was a big lift to his campaign," Elefante, now 78, recalled today. "From that day on, he always referred to Utica as his good luck charm."

Yesterday, Elefante received a payment of sorts for his work on Roosevelt's behalf. Gov. Carey named him one of 80 members of a special state commission to commemorate FDR's centennial.

He joined the likes of newsman Walter Cronkite, Pulitzer Prize winning author and historian Arthur Schlesinger, Sen. Daniel Patrick Moynihan and dozens more of the state's most prominent citizens on the panel.

ELEFANTE

"It was like a reunion," Elefante said of yesterday's gathering in Albany. "A lot of the old gang was there. Guys like Billy McKeon (former state Democratic chairman from Auburn) and Erastus Corning (Albany mayor). Roosevelt's son (Franklin Jr.) came up and put his arms around me and game me a hug."

In 1928, Elefante was beginning his ascent to power in state politics. He was working under William Bray, the Oneida County and state Democratic chairman.

"Let me give you a little history," Elefante said today. "I'll go back in my memory a little."

Rufie Elefante remembers a lot about Roosevelt, the governor, and Roosevelt, the four-term president. But ask him about dates and he waves his hand in disgust.

"I've been playing this game for too many years to remember dates," he said. "I never kept any records. I always played day-to-day."

When the Democrats nominated Al Smith for president in 1928, state party leaders, led by Bray and a group

(See FDR — Page 10)

NEW YORK STATE
FRANKLIN DELANO ROOSEVELT
CENTENNIAL COMMISSION
Hugh L. Carey, Governor

Arthur Schlesinger, Jr.
Chairman

Fredrica S. Goodman
Executive Director

Honorary Chairmen:

Benjamin V. Cohen
Erastus Corning, II
*David Dubinsky
W. Averell Harriman
Anna Rosenberg Hoffman
Jacob K. Javits
Vernon E. Jordan, Jr.
John J. McCloy
Daniel Patrick Moynihan
William S. Paley
Mrs. Nelson Rockefeller
Mrs. John A. Roosevelt
Franklin D. Roosevelt, Jr.
Mrs. Samuel Rosenman
Robert F. Wagner
Thomas Watson

Members:

Joseph Alsop
Gordon M. Ambach
Lauren Bacall
Herman Badillo
Dominic Baranello
Carol Bellamy
Beatrice Berle
Jonathan Bingham
John Brademas
Rabbi Balfour Brickner
James MacGregor Burns
Schuyler Chapin
*John Cheever
Kenneth Clark
Betty Comden
Walter Cronkite
Peter Crotty
Sol Chaikin
Tom Cuite
Margaret Truman Daniel
Charles Dyson
Rufus P. Elefante
Osborn Elliott
Ralph Ellison
William Emerson
James Emery
Barry Feinstein
Justin Feldman
Stanley Fink
Murray H. Finley
Hamilton Fish, Jr.
Richard M. Flynn
Michael Forrestal
Dixon B. Freeland
Richard Gardner
Lloyd Garrison
Victor Gotbaum
Henry Graff
Adolph Green
Armand Hammer
Raymond B. Harding
Louis Harris
Kitty Carlisle Hart
John Jay Iselin
Bernard K. Johnpoll
Richard Kahan
Eugene Keogh
Arthur Krim
Joseph Lash
Mary Lasker
Orin Lehman
Louis Lefkowitz
William Leuchtenburg
Carol Lubin
Sidney Lumet
Vincent Marchiselli
John P. McGrath
William H. McKeon
*William Morgan
Henry Morgenthau
Robert Morgenthau
Manfred Ohrenstein
Richard Ottinger
Frederick Papert
Joseph Papp
Basil Paterson
Justine Wise Polier
Peter Quinn
Charles Rangel
Richard Ravitch
Mildred and Louis Resnick
Joseph Robinson
David Rockefeller
Felix Rohatyn
Marvin Rosenberg
Dorothy Schiff
Abba Schwartz
Beverly Sills
Steven Smith
Michael Sovern
Ronald Stack
Roger Stevens
John S. Stillman
Marietta Tree
Brian Urquhart
Harry Van Arsdale
Cyrus Vance
William J. vanden Heuvel
Richard Wade
William Walton
James Wechsler
Clifton R. Wharton, Jr.
Theodore H. White
Malcolm Wilson

Deceased

For Further Information: FDR Centennial Commission
4 Burnett Boulevard
Poughkeepsie, New York 12603
(914) 473-8151

Arthur Schlesinger, Jr., Chairman
New York State
Franklin D. Roosevelt Centennial Commission
and
William J. vanden Heuvel, President
Four Freedoms Foundation
request the pleasure of your company
at the presentation of
Franklin D. Roosevelt Freedom Medals
to
Averell Harriman

Jacob K. Javits
Coretta Scott King
Robert S. McNamara
Joseph L. Rauh, Jr.
Friday, March 4, 1983
Eleven o'clock
St. James' Church
Hyde Park, New York

Please reply by
February 15, 1983

Governor and Mrs. Mario M. Cuomo
cordially invite you to
"An Old Fashioned Barbecue"
honoring the
New York State Democratic Committee
on
Thursday, August 8, 1985
6:00-9:00 p.m.
Executive Mansion
Albany, New York

Kindly reply by July 31st
and indicate the name of your guest.

(914) 431-5913 Mailed 7/29/85 *Dress Informal*

Water, water everywhere... and who has paid the price?

By RUFUS P. ELEFANTE

■ GUEST COLUMN

I would like to acquaint the representatives of the towns and villages with some of the pertinent facts concerning the Board of Water Supply prior to the meeting called by Chairman Robert Pierce for Feb. 26 at City Hall.

In 1937, a committee of outstanding businessmen from the City of Utica was named by Mayor Vincent Corrou to examine and review the purchase of the Consolidated Water Company, now known as the Utica Water Board.

ELEFANTE

After serious consideration and investigation, the Commission decided to recommend to the Utica Common Council the purchase of the Consolidated Water Company for $7.9 million. In order to commence the procedures to purchase the water company, a special act of the state Legislature was required which would grant the City permission to purchase the company. This enabling legislation was passed.

At this time, Utica had reached its bonded debt limit. There was no way for the city to issue bonds to purchase the water company. Charles Donnelley (a former Utica postmaster) and I went to Washington and enlisted the aid of our close personal friend, the late United States senator, James M. Mead of New York. Sen. Mead took both of us to the Reconstruction Finance Corporation established by President Roosevelt. We made an agreement with the Reconstruction Finance Corporation for the city of Utica that would permit the city to issue revenue sharing bonds at 3 percent for the $7.9 million purchase price. This was accomplished without any guarantees by the Utica taxpayers.

The Common Council with the bipartisan cooperation of the Democrat majority leader, the late Daniel M. Laino, and Republican minority leader, the late Charles A. Thomas, unanimously passed legislation to purchase the water company with the condition that no taxes would be paid on water company properties anywhere.

Twenty years after this agreement was passed, the towns had the Republican state Legislature and the late Gov. Thomas E. Dewey sign a law which enabled the towns and villages to tax the water company properties in their towns and villages respectively. This act by Gov. Dewey and the Republican state Legislature cost the water company over $10 million dollars in taxes, thereby making it impossible for the company to make the necessary long-term improvements to the water company system. The Town of New Hartford enjoyed rapid growth, prosperity and the creation of many water districts. With this population growth, a serious problem on water pressure was being created for the people the water district was serving. We called a Water Board meeting with the Town of New Hartford chaired by Supervisor Gordon Newell.

We explained to the New Hartford officials that because of New Hartford's rapid growth the town would need water tanks, pipes and pumping stations that would cost between $1½ and 2 million dollars to build up water pressure. We also told him that New Hartford was reaping a tremendous amount of money from property taxes, with its growth and the water it was receiving from the city of Utica. This water asset was making it possible for them to receive huge tax dollars and therefore they could pay for the improvements to the system they were enjoying because they were reaping the tax dollars and not Utica, who owned the water company.

They refused!

Thomas Acres (a housing development), then applied for a water district and was purposely refused. A water company action to increase the rates followed by a lawsuit ensued as a result. The lawsuit was won by the city of Utica and it resulted in the towns getting a 32% increase in their water rate.

It was truly unfortunate that the towns joined up with New Hartford in the water rate case, because the towns, in doing so, were subject to the DEC (Department of Environmental Conservation) decision of the same 32% increase on the water rate that was given to New Hartford. It is especially unfortunate because most of the towns' growth and expansion was nil. The only real growth in the area was the town of New Hartford which should have actually paid legally and morally for the improvements to the water system since it reaped the tax revenues and no one else.

Rufus P. Elefante is commissioner of the Utica Board of Water Supply and a long-time Utica Democratic leader.

History has its place, too, in the pages of the present

Published on the next page is an essay by Rufus P. Elefante about the Utica Board of Water Supply. Longtime readers of the Observer-Dispatch may be puzzled about the newspaper's giving Elefante space for the second time in three weeks. As a powerful figure in the Democratic Party, he has been articulate for five decades or more in criticizing the Daily Press and Observer-Dispatch.

MCMILLAN

Freedom of the press, guaranteed by the First Amendment to the U.S. Constitution, belongs to all the people, however, not just to companies that own printing presses. Thus, I think it appropriate for Elefante, if he wishes, to share his opinions through the city's Sunday newspaper.

More significant than this exercise in First Amendment doctrine, however, is Elefante's message. While I believe it must be discounted in terms of making public policy for the 1990's, it must not be ignored.

The message, basically, is that history cannot be overlooked.

Both in conversation and in print, Elefante is fiercely proud of Utica's success under his leadership in getting the municipal water supply into public ownership during the Great Depression. The health of that water system, in turn, permitted the astonishing growth that Utica's suburbs have experienced in the last three decades.

JOHN H. McMILLAN

Neither Utica nor Elefante, however, received gratitude from the suburbs. Instead, the Republican towns and villages saw the Board of Water Supply as a source for tax revenue, and recent history has been marked by court fights over water rates.

When Elefante's essay arrived at the newspaper last week, one editor argued against using it. "He's writing about history," the editor said. A newspaper is supposed to deal with current events, the argument went, not the sins and achievements of the past.

That's a major problem of the U.S. news business, in my view. We report events without providing the context from which those events developed. As a result, the men and women who make public policy tend to ignore precedent and experience.

It's impossible, for example, to make any sense of President Reagan's anti-communism without understanding his experiences in the 1950s as head of an actors' union. Russia's behavior relates in many ways to the devastation it experienced in World War II. The U.S. commitment to Israel relates directly to guilt about the Holocaust and American inaction in the face of Hitler's terror. The policy of affirmative action is justified by conditions for blacks before Brown vs. Board of Education in the 1950s.

So it is with the history of the American city. The boomers built our cities and then, after World War II, used the cities as their financial bases from which to build the suburbs. Suburban shopping centers destroyed scores of downtown shopping districts. Arterial highways, constructed to speed suburbanites from their homes to their jobs, ripped up ethnic neighborhoods that had taken generations to create.

It's not surprising, therefore, that men and women who invested their lives in a community are less than enthusiastic about the current enthusiasm for regional solutions and regional control of agencies like the water board.

To fresh eyes, of course, Utica and Rome look like one city. In a perfect world, the two cities and their suburbs would share police and fire departments, school systems, Chambers of Commerce, United Way organizations and health services.

The current structure of both government and non-profit agencies is hideously expensive in duplicated bureaucracies and services. Fortunately, some progress has been made — in mass transit, waste management, the Boy Scouts, siting of SUNY's technical college between the two cities, and the like. Nevertheless, regionalization moves glacially.

It's customary to claim that the problem is the resistance of key players, defending narrow interests, to surrendering power. That's only partly true. The reality is that the nation's cities, including Utica, have been exploited in years gone by. Land developers, builders and all of us who created suburbia made lots of money because cities had gone before. To expect city folk to forget is to pretend the moon is blue, and I'm glad Elefante's essay reminds us of that.

John H. McMillan is publisher of the Observer-Dispatch and the Daily Press.

Rufus P. Elefante Associates

Genesee-Watson Building
1508-1512 Genesee Street
Utica, New York 13502
Telephone (315) 724-0855
Exchange (315) 724-9411

Rufus P. Elefante, President
Joseph Alberico, Secretary

February 25, 1986

Mr. John D. McMillan
Publisher - Observer Dispatch
Gannett Newspaper
221 Oriskany Plaza
Utica, New York 13501

Dear Sir:

The article appearing in Sunday's newspaper with your by-line cast a ray of hope for the people of this area. At last this area will have an honest newspaper.

Your quote on the right of freedom of the press belonging to all the people was a right denied to the people over the past fifty years by the local press. The contents of your statement were excellent and true.

I am truly appreciative of this and I thank you for allowing me the guest column for the first time in my life.

Sincerely,

Rufus P. Elefante

Rufus P. Elefante

The Observer-Dispatch

■ 10/Friday, February 28, 1986

Opinion

■ Tomorrow:
■ Kilpatrick's conservative view
■ The world of Doonesbury
■ What do you think?

■ EDITORIAL

Elefante is right on regional responsibilities

John McMillan
Publisher
792-5003

Jack Marsh
Executive Editor
792-5004

Anthony Vella
Managing Editor
792-5008

Michael J. Woods
Editorial Page Editor
792-5006

When members of the Utica Board of Water Supply met with representatives of area suburbs Wednesday night, one of the main topics of conversation was the possibility of forming a regional water authority.

Board Chairman Robert Pierce had called the meeting in hopes of fostering greater cooperation between the city water board and the towns and villages it serves. A regional water system could go a long way toward achieving that goal.

In the past, as area residents are well aware, there has been much wrangling between city and suburbs over water issues such as rates and expansion of service to outlying areas.

The city-run board has been viewed by some suburban leaders as operating in a rather dictatorial fashion. For their part, water commissioners have argued they were merely protecting the city's interests.

Now, the makeup of the five-member water board has changed due to the appointment of three new members by Mayor Louis LaPolla. This has opened the door to new attitudes and hopeful dialogue.

Wednesday's meeting went well. There was a broad exchange of views, and future sessions no doubt will be held to pursue greater cooperation leading perhaps to a regional authority.

That is all well and good. As Herkimer County Legislator John Brezinski, D-8, said at the meeting, progress will be made in Utica and its suburbs only through cooperation and regional efforts.

It should be remembered, however, that cooperation is a two-way street. Water Board Commissioner Rufus Elefante, a non-LaPolla appointee who has opposed regionalizing the water system, had some interesting things to say about that during the meeting.

He suggested that if suburban leaders want to have a greater say in water matters, they should pursue the same logic with regard to other regional issues. He is right.

Water is just one of many regional topics that should be discussed among city, suburban and county leaders.

Elefante noted that Utica, like many other cities, is struggling financially, even while it tries to support what are properly regional amenities such as the auditorium, library and zoo.

What Elefante is saying is quite simple, and it makes sense. If the towns and villages want to share responsibility for the water system, they also should be willing to assume greater responsibility for other regional facilities run by the city.

The rationale for establishing a regional water authority is no different from the rationale for seeking greater regional involvement (including financial support) with regard to the auditorium, zoo and library. After all, suburbanites enjoy those facilities, too, while the city pays the lion's share of the upkeep.

As Elefante said, the towns and villages should appeal to their county legislators, seeking more countywide help for all of Utica's "regional" facilities.

The concept of regional government is becoming more and more appealing as smaller government units face hard fiscal times. Water is just one of the issues that need to be discussed.

Sunday Observer-Dispatch/Gary Fountain

ELEFANTE AT 83 — "I'm sort of a clean-living guy. I never did anything to excess, let me put it that way. I could have caviar if I wanted, but I'm just an ordinary guy. I'd rather have pasta and beans anyday, between you and me."

Elefante calls 'em as he sees 'em

By MARJ PATRICK

Utica Democratic leader Rufus P. Elefante's talk with a reporter last week was wide-ranging. Among his comments on many subjects:

Utica Board of Water Supply: Engineering Utica's purchase of the private water company in 1938 was "the greatest thing I ever did." It cost $7.8 million and he estimates it's now worth $30 million. It was purchased with help of President Franklin Roosevelt's Reconstruction Finance Corp., so the bonds were backed by the water board's assets "without one nickel of the city's credit behind it."

Reason he was appointed a water board commissioner: "(Mayor Edward) Hanna (who had been feuding with the Press and Observer-Dispatch) appointed me to spite the Utica newspapers." Elefante resigned last Tuesday, in protest over the board's settlement of the Hampton Heights lawsuit filed by Albert Fraccola Jr.

On prejudice: Politics helped the Italian-Americans gain respect in Utica. "We were Italian-Americans and we were looked at as third-class citizens. We worked to be first-class citizens where we belonged. That was my ambition."

Best Utica mayor: The late Charles Donnelley, his political mentor and friend.

Best Utica-area assemblyman: "My godson, Richard Ruggiero." Ruggiero resigned earlier this year after pleading guilty to a felony: attempted sexual abuse. "Too bad he got into this mess."

Best New York State governor: Skipping over Franklin D. Roosevelt, he said Herbert Lehman, 1933-42, "a great humanitarian, a great governor who liked us and did a lot of nice things for Oneida County."

On East Utica Democratic politics: "East Utica was solidly Republican" during his early political years. In part, he attributes the switch to Democrat by his Italian-American friends and neighbors to the 1928 election. He said they were unhappy at the charges thrown at fellow Catholic, Democrat Alfred E. Smith, during his unsuccessful bid for president.

On being investigated: "Two investigations came and I was clean as a hound's tooth so I must tell you anything I did was on the up and up and was honest." He said his references were to what he called a Republican-inspired 1949 vote probe in which he and 16 other Democrats were indicted, then later acquitted and to the 1957 Fischer investigation. He said he also went out of his way to pay income taxes because "that's the only way they get a politician."

On his political leadership: "I did not look at myself as a boss. I thought of myself as a person who loved the city and wanted to help." Also: "How can I say I'm a leader when I've never been elected (party chairman)? I'm a 'de facto' leader."

On helping the Utica area: He said he worked with fellow Democrats to bring many tangible assets to the area — especially during the Depression when the construction projects provided needed jobs. Although many Republicans and some Democrats would dispute his list, he includes many projects, including the water board; Griffiss Air Force Base in Rome (he originally hoped it could go in Deerfield but army engineers thought that was too hilly); the Sheraton Inn and Conference Center; the Municipal Housing Authority projects for low-income people; the State University College of Technology and the Utica golf course designed by the top golf course architect, Robert Trent Jones.

Sunday O-D 12 March 1989 P 3C

Elefante's leadership deserves praise

With regard to the Rufus Elefante saga, I for one am a great admirer of Mr. Elefante and it gripes me to hear today's young Italian-Americans make disparaging remarks about his so-called bossism.

Most of us older Italian-Americans who suffered through the Depression owe a debt of gratitude to him. Mr. Elefante looked out for us when no one else cared. Things were tough. There were no jobs and money was scarce, but somehow we were able to earn a few dollars by cleaning the city streets, cleaning snow downtown, collecting trash for the Laino Brothers, or sweeping the floors at the old Foster Brothers.

The younger Italian-Americans never knew what hard times were; they never felt the prejudicial attitudes against us.

It was because of Mr. Elefante that we were able to help our children to become today's doctors, lawyers, dentists, teachers, and leaders.

I was especially surprised to read of Angelo Amodio's remark, "They ruined everything they got their hands on," of course meaning Mr. Elefante, since Mr. Amodio's background is East Utican.

I have been all over the world. Most of the places I have been to make Utica appear like the Vatican in comparison.

THOMAS CANTORE
Utica

Utica politics — look to the future

Alan Ehrenhalt's article on Utica's political history in the current issue of Governing magazine appears to agree with past written interpretations.

The fact that many of the persons involved in Utica administrations were of Italian descent does not cast aspersions upon the entire Italian-American community as Joe Testa implies in his statement.

As a native of another state who has resided here for nearly 17 years, I can attest to the fact that the Utica area has much to offer in its quality of life, is constantly improving, and has a future to which we can look forward.

Let us view history for what it's worth, a view of the past. It has occurred, we should study it, and we should attempt to interpret it.

But isn't it the future in which we should all be interested and work for?

If we can learn to be forward looking and not let past events bother us and create controversy, we can be assured that our community will become an even better place in which to live.

JOHN LEVITAS
19C Sadaquada Apts., Whitesboro

LETTERS TO THE EDITOR

'Old political ways' brought progress

Last week in an article appearing in the Utica newspapers, there was the usual derogatory slant on the "old ways of politics."

ELEFANTE

Did the reporter mean the people who brought the Rome Air Base here?

Or did the reporter mean the people who bought the Water Company for the people of Utica without a penny of taxpayer's money?

Did the reporter mean the people who brought General Electric here?

Did he mean those who brought millions of dollars in WPA Projects that built so many things in the community that Uticans have and enjoy?

Did the reporter mean the people who brought the State University College of Technology here?

Did he mean the people who were instrumental in getting the $100 million MUD Project currently under construction here?

Or did the reporter mean the same men that J. David Hogue, a former publisher and editor of the Utica papers prevailed upon to help establish the present Oneida County Airport?

RUFUS P. ELEFANTE
1508-1512 Genesee St., Utica

NICHOLAS ACOCELLA

POLITICS

PANCAKE HOUSE POLITICKING

If you need a favor in Utica, New York, don't go to the party clubhouse or city hall, go to Uncle Henry's Restaurant.

Utica, New York, a mill town that once flourished on cheap Italian labor, had to find a new industry when J.P. Stevens and other textile firms moved to the South in search of even cheaper labor in the 1950s. So it was that Utica became Sin City.

The town went wide open. Virtually every resident over 40 can point out where the best gambling spots were, where after-hours joints thrived, where fancy bordellos prospered—all under the eye of an insouciant police department. (The police chief admitted that he had kept one brothel under surveillance for 20 years without gathering enough evidence to make a single arrest.) Organized crime overran Utica. Thirteen unsolved gangland slayings cluttered the books. A disproportionate number of participants at the Apalachin, New York, conclave of organized crime's high command hailed from Utica. Even the notorious Albert Anastasia of Murder Incorporated dabbled in Utica's gambling operations.

The excitement didn't last. Like an old rake with nothing left but his memories, Utica settled down and became just another tired industrial snowbelt city of 85,000 people (more than 40 percent of them Italian Americans). What did not settle down was Rufus Elefante.

Rufie, as everyone calls him, is the most powerful man in the city, even though he has never held—or coveted—any office but the unofficial one of Democratic leader.

Twice daily, at 11 AM and 7 PM with a nap in between, Rufie (rhyming vaguely with Duffy), holds court in an unprepossessing downtown eatery called Uncle Henry's Pancake Restaurant, from which he dispenses political wisdom and favors. The restaurant is surrounded by three parking lots, presumably to accommodate Rufie's guests, who may on any given day include former mayors, local attorneys, Board of Education officials, labor leaders, city employees, and Rufie's grandson. With no available telephone other than the pay booth at Uncle Henry's, the waitresses serve as receptionists, summoning him to the phone and announcing the steady flow of visitors one unfriendly Democrat calls "Rufie's altar boys." Uncle Henry's is Rufie's one and only office.

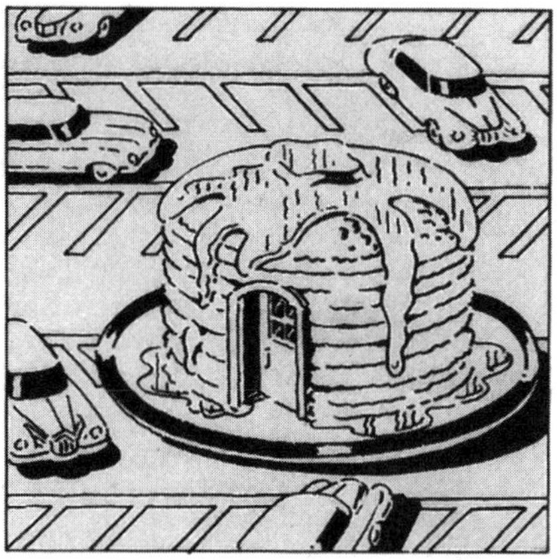

ELEFANTE'S FEUDS AND FAVORS

The ghosts of old politics hover about this Rufie-dominated restaurant. The formica echoes with stories, whispered and shouted: Al Smith's feud with William Gibbs McAdoo over the Ku Klux Klan; the rally of 10,000 that Rufie staged for Roosevelt; Rufie's battles with Jim Farley over party endorsements; and his endless arguments with Governor Averell Harriman.

The nostalgia is only background. It should not mislead anyone into believing the daily gatherings at Uncle Henry's are all reminiscences. Rufie remains an active politician and his power, however mercurial, remains intact. He still turns out thousands of votes, seemingly with a nod of his head. He still inspires fear, distaste, even amusement in local politicians, though none spurn his support.

In the opinion of Mike Caruso, a former Republican mayor, Rufie is "sharper and more astute today than ever before." He is, in any case, one of the last of a near-extinct species of political animal, the urban boss.

Rufie's power dates back to the late 1920s when Italians were the objects of discrimination in Utica. "In those days," he says, "everything was 'Wop, wop, wop.' I got into politics to help Italians."

Some claim Rufie's political mastery did indeed help Italians. His supporters remember that his clout brought jobs to the city and "put bread on our table." Others, however, say Italians would have prospered anyway and that, even if Rufie helped people, he did even better for himself.

Rufie, a former truck driver, translated the large majorities he turned out for Roosevelt into several lucrative government hauling contracts. Investing wisely, mostly in real estate, he became wealthy enough to engage in politics full time.

Today he deals exclusively in deals. About current contracts he is reticent. But, apparently observing a self-imposed statute of limitations, he is candid about the past, telling remarkable tales of political machinations. A particular favorite is how he cast a vote for Lyndon Johnson at the 1960 Democratic National Convention to repay a Brooklyn congressman who had appointed a deserving Utican to West Point.

Most of Rufie's stories, of course, concern his victories and triumphs which made possible the favors that in turn created more votes with which to win new political battles.

Utica benefited. During the Depression, Rufie's Washington connections brought jobs. When the mills left in the 1940s, Rufie pulled a few strings and brought Griffiss Air Force Base to the county. He helped convince giant corporations like General Electric, Bendix, and Chicago Pneumatic Tool to locate plants in the area. Oneida County Democratic Chairman Ray Stefano credits Rufie, with whom he frequently feuds, with spurring the "loom to boom" transformation of Utica.

Nevertheless, both Rufie and Utica

ILLUSTRATION BY GEORGE MAS

From "Attenzione" magazine

FRIENDS OF SENATOR D'AMATO
P.O. BOX 1000
MINEOLA, NEW YORK 11501

June 15, 1988

Dear Rufus,

Many thanks for your generous support. Your efforts in making our luncheon in Utica a great success are deeply appreciated. It was a terrific event and I enjoyed myself tremendously.

We must continue to struggle to restore a legitimate government in Panama and to end the control of Manuel Noriega and his massive drug trafficking operation. With your continued support, I will strive to restore the death penalty for those druglords who commit murder in pursuit of their own interests. Fortunately, I was able to pass this legislation in the Senate but it's up to all of us to get this legislation passed in the House.

Again, let me express my heartfelt thanks for your ongoing friendship and confidence.

Warmest personal regards,

Al

Alfonse M. D'Amato
United States Senator

AMD:nk

Paid for by Friends of Senator D'Amato

HAMILTON COLLEGE
Clinton, New York 13323

Department of Sociology

January 25, 1990

Rufus Elefante
1508 Genesee St.
Utica, NY 13502

Dear Mr. Elefante:

I was mayor of the City of Burlington, Vermont from 1981 to 1989. I am presently a Visiting Professor of Sociology at Hamilton College and am teaching a course in Urban Problems.

The role that you have played in Utica politics and city government is well known throughout the country by those of us interested in local politics. While I am in the Utica area I was wondering if it would be possible for me to invite you to lunch in order to chat for a while about some of your recollections regarding city, state and national politics.

I will give you a ring next week and see if we can work out a mutually convenient time. I look forward to meeting with you.

Sincerely,

Bernard Sanders

S:j

Presently a Senator from Vermont

GOVERNING

The States and Localities

Jan. 3, 1989

Dr. Angela M. Elefante
Columbus School
Utica N.Y.

Dear Dr. Elefante:

I hope it is not presumptuous to come to you out of the blue with a request for a favor. I am political editor of Governing Magazine, a Washington-based monthly specializing in the politics and problems of America's states and cities.

At the moment, I am working on an article about Utica, as part of a series on political changes in a number of communities around the country over the past generation. It will be published in the March issue of Governing. Early in December, I spent a week in Utica talking to various political leaders past and present. I very much wanted to meet with your father, but he was recovering from surgery that week and I did not want to disturb him.

As I complete work on the article, however, it seems a shame not to have his comments on the political history of Utica in modern times. I would be more than happy to return to the city for an interview at any time that he found convenient. I have been unable to reach him at his office, and hoped it might be feasible to contact him through you.

I am enclosing a copy of Governing so that you will see it is a serious magazine that portrays political issues thoroughly and accurately. I have no axe to grind and no prejudices against any of the city's political leaders. The fact is, Rufus Elefante is an important figure in 20th century urban history, and his views are important for posterity.

If his health does not permit an interview, or if he would rather not participate, I will understand. But I thought it only fair for me to offer him an opportunity to be heard, since so much of the article inevitably will revolve around his years of work in Utica public life.

I will call in a day or two to see if something might be arranged. If you wish, you may call me at (202) 822-1410. Once again, I apologize for troubling you.

Sincerely,

Alan Ehrenhalt

Alan Ehrenhalt
Governing Magazine

A Congressional Quarterly Publication
1414 22nd Street N.W. • Washington, D.C. 20037 • (202) 887-6261

UTICA, NEW YORK

THE RISE AND FALL OF A HAUGHTY POLITICAL MACHINE

Rufie Elefante is the boss Utica no longer wants but hasn't learned to live without.

By Alan Ehrenhalt

To understand Utica politics, it helps to know something about Utica restaurants.

In the beginning, there was Marino's. Utica has always had a city hall, but for more than two decades after World War II, Marino's was the real seat of government, the place where Rufus Elefante's Democratic machine dispensed favors and made the decisions that kept the town going. It was an old-fashioned Italian restaurant crowded with high-backed wooden booths, and the booth a customer chose often depended on the sort of help he wanted. There was one for jobs, one for welfare complaints, one for city contracts, each booth maintained by an Elefante lieutenant. A businessman who wanted a building permit was sometimes advised to head for Marino's back room, join a card game with some of Rufie's boys and lose as much money as possible.

After Marino's fell victim to the wrecking ball in 1972, there was Uncle Henry's Pancake House. Few went there for the food; old-timers remember it as ranging between mediocre and inedible. There were those, in fact, who doubted whether pancakes were "Uncle Henry" Cittadino's true calling. They remembered his conviction in 1959 on charges of running a brothel. Nevertheless, Uncle Henry's was Elefante's main political meeting place for years after Marino's was gone. The waitresses there spent more time taking Rufie's messages than they did serving food.

Wherever the lunch took place, the meetings often adjourned to a more private spot after the meal was over. On days when the city's common council met, Elefante liked to finish eating, then take off for a drive with the city clerk to instruct him on how the council meeting was to proceed.

Uncle Henry's has gone the way of Marino's, and it has had no successor. There is no power restaurant in Utica anymore. And for a good reason: There isn't much power. Five years ago, the Utica *Observer-Dispatch* sent one of its reporters on an extended assignment to determine the city's top 10 power brokers. He managed to come up with only three names. That was not because he found a sinister triumvirate running the city. It was because he couldn't detect anyone else with a broad-ranging influence over local affairs.

Utica has humbled its haughty Democratic machine. The machine is not dead: Elefante, still active at 85, can make life very difficult for any local Democratic candidate he does not like. But outside the confines of his shrinking territory on the Italian east side, Elefante cannot elect anyone anymore. His support is now a burden for any candidate running citywide. All the important positions in Utica politics have been lost to the Republicans. And all the power that Elefante's machine once held seems to have evaporated.

Presiding at city hall in his third term is Mayor Louis D. LaPolla, a man who is tireless, incorruptible and, when it comes to using raw political power, as innocent as a lamb. Seven of the nine members of the Utica common council are Republicans, like LaPolla, but he has no steady influence over the votes of any of them.

By and large, Utica is glad it abandoned machine rule, and there is no evidence that it would like to go back. Still, one doesn't have to search very far to find a few traces of nostalgia. "If you want things to happen," says Utica College political scientist Richard Emmert, "the pieces have to be put together. Rufie controlled the mayor, he controlled the council, he put them together. Nobody can

Rufus P. Elefante is still active at 85, but his support has become a burden for any candidate who is running citywide. 'I worked for Utica,' he insists. 'Please believe me. I loved my Italian people. I wanted them to progress.'

do that now."

The decline of political machines is old news these days in America. But the question of how to govern in their absence remains crucial in many cities, big ones like Chicago and Philadelphia and smaller ones like Utica.

In virtually all of these places, machines have fallen apart for the same familiar reasons: the departure of the immigrant generation that depended on them for jobs; the influence of the media in determining elections; the distaste of a more affluent, educated electorate for any political system that thrives on graft.

In all the important respects, Utica's Democratic machine was a fairly typical one. What is fascinating about it is the hold that it has on the mind of the community, years after it lost any real authority over city affairs. Rufie Elefante is the political boss Utica no longer wants but hasn't learned to live without.

Rufus P. Elefante has never been elected to office. He has never been an important official of the Democratic Party, either in the city of Utica or surrounding Oneida County. He has been in trucking, wrecking and real estate, but not public office. "Office-holders are baby kissers," he says scornfully. "I was never that kind."

Nevertheless, he came to dominate the city, starting in the simplest possible way, gathering up as many votes as he could find in the Italian neighborhoods and trading them for favors from party leaders citywide. In 1928, he made a brilliant decision: He invested the influence he had in the gubernatorial campaign of Franklin Delano Roosevelt. Elefante staged a huge rally for FDR at the corner of Mohawk and Bleecker streets, in the heart of Utica's Little Italy. It came at a time when most of the other upstate cities were giving the candidate a cool

Lawrence Mason Jr. photographs

At last, nation will see balanced picture of Utica

George Newman

For a city of its size, Utica has been the object of a fair amount of national attention — most of it less than flattering and much of it inaccurate.

Now a magazine called "Governing," published by Congressional Quarterly Inc., has produced a comprehensive, balanced account of what Utica is all about.

The article — most of which appears elsewhere in this newspaper — is no puff piece. Author Alan Ehrenhalt, the magazine's political editor, describes the "Sin City" days of the 1940s and '50s. He recounts most of the city's troubles during and after state investigations of municipal corruption. He concludes that "incessant bickering" is the dominant feature of Utica's political scene.

But Ehrenhalt also sees Utica as a community that works, "one that provides comfort and stability to those within it." He recognizes the value of a city in which "citizens know one another, and their parents know one another, and their children know one another."

"Governing," of course, is not a journal of sociology. It is devoted to state and local politics. The focus of Ehrenhalt's article is the Rufus Elefante political machine — what it meant to the city in its heyday and what its decline means today.

Ehrenhalt's findings are not startling. The machine, he writes, collapsed for the same reasons similar organizations evaporated in Chicago and Philadelphia: A principal cause was "the departure of the immigrant generation that depended on (the machine) for jobs."

It isn't remarkable that Ehrenhalt managed to relate Utica's politics to the national picture; finding larger meanings in local government is what his magazine is all about. But it is noteworthy that he managed to avoid the hyperbole and caricature that has marked much national reporting about Utica.

He quotes a 1958 example from Newsweek: "Utica is the town the gangsters own. ... It is the headquarters town for the big-time mobster operations in most of the eastern half of the nation."

I wasn't around here in those days, but everything I've learned suggests that Utica was at most a Mafia substation; the local leaders reported to chieftains in Buffalo. Crime and corruption certainly were rampant here, but the "headquarters town for big-time mobster operations" was the one in which Newsweek is published: New York City.

Ehrenhalt also makes a passing reference to former Mayor Edward A. Hanna and his predecessor, Richard Assaro:

"After the Republican (Frank) Dulan left the mayoralty in 1967," Ehrenhalt wrote, (Utica politics) produced a reform-minded liberal Democrat ... followed by a cantankerous independent who declared his hatred for politics of all sorts. Both prided themselves on their freedom from machine control, and both were failures."

My first job at this newspaper was City Hall reporter when Hanna was mayor. I spent a lot of time talking to out-of-town writers who had been assigned to tell the world about Utica's unusual mayor. Their portraits always turned out to be one-dimensional: Most often Hanna was a hero fighting the city's establishment. Sometimes he was just a fascinating eccentric.

Ultimately Hanna was indeed a failure, as Ehrenhalt says, because he was driven more by his ego than by a sense of public service. If Hanna reads Ehrenhalt's piece, he will be most bothered, I suspect, by the omission of his name.

In a telephone conversation, Ehrenhalt confirms that he found Utica a fascinating place. He plans a book on urban politics in which Utica's story will be a chapter — at about twice the length of the magazine article.

I thought the one gap in the article was its non-mention of the dispute over Utica schools, which threatens the sense of community that Ehrenhalt found remarkable. He said, however, that a discussion of the school situation had been edited out for space reasons.

The school question will be in the book. If the entire volume is as insightful as Ehrenhalt's view of Utica, it will deserve wide success.

George Newman is associate editor of the Observer-Dispatch, 221 Oriskany Plaza, Utica, N.Y. 13501. His column appears every Sunday.

Elefante machine ran Utica better, readers tell O-D

By PAT LOUISE
Observer-Dispatch

By an almost 2-to-1 margin, most callers in a special Observer-Dispatch survey believe Utica would be better off under machine-style politics instead of independent government.

Approximately 150 people called the O-D Tuesday to talk about a chapter on the city in Alan Ehrenhalt's book, "The United States of Ambition." The newspaper published the chapter Sunday through Tuesday.

The actual count was 90 for and 48 against machine rule. The results were adjusted to eliminate calls by the same person and multiple calls with identical wording. That occurred for both answers to the question.

Ehrenhalt wrote about the influence of longtime Democratic leader Rufus Elefante and the city's political history since his rise in the 1940s. Ehrenhalt compared Elefante's style with that of Mayor Louis D. LaPolla, whom he terms an independent politician.

At the end of the chapter, Ehrenhalt leaves open his answer about which method served Utica better. The O-D survey asked readers their opinions on Utica politics.

One caller seemed to sum up the thoughts of those who backed independent government. "We are more independent today and we don't owe loyalty to anyone. It's

See MACHINE, Page 2A

CRUMBS ALONG THE MOHAWK — **By Randall Kimberly**

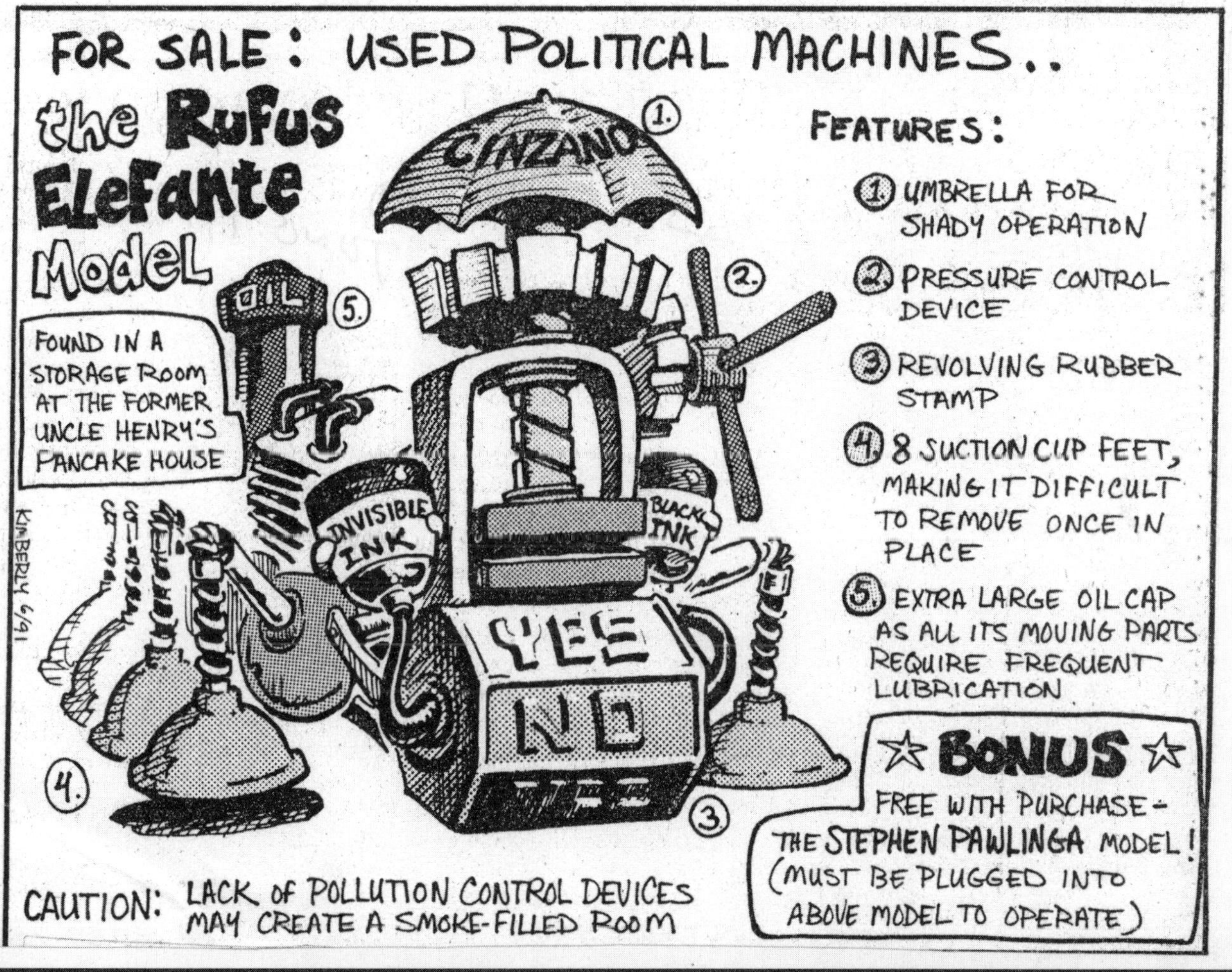

 Utica, N.Y., Sunday, May 31, 1992

Rufus Elefante remembers

Photo by Michael Doherty

Rufus Elefante in his Genesee Street office recently.

Former Utica 'boss' looks back — and ahead

By MICHAEL J. WOODS
Observer-Dispatch

In his first in-depth public discussion in more than five years, longtime political leader Rufus P. Elefante said he is pessimistic about Utica's future and its current political leaders.

"The city is in terrible shape, and nobody knows where it is going," said Elefante, who directed Utica's Democratic political machine for more than a quarter of a century from a booth in a restaurant.

"In my day, we knew where we wanted to go ... we had the connections," he said during a wide-ranging interview. "The difference today is that the leaders don't know how to do it ... they don't understand politics."

Elefante, one of the last of the old-time political bosses, was the unelected mayor of all he surveyed in the '30s, '40s and '50s. As de facto leader of city Democrats, and as master-weaver of political debts and IOUs, he had a grip on City Hall that was iron-clad.

After a state probe of city government in the late '50s and early '60s, the monolithic power of Elefante's political machine was broken. Yet he continued to be a force for three more decades.

Today, at age 89, he says "the vim and the fire are gone," indicating that he isn't very much involved in politics anymore.

But his animated commentary, much of it devoted to a spirited defense of the days — and the ways — he ran Utica, belied that cold-embered self-assessment.

Dapper in a blue suit, red-and-blue tie, red suspenders and a white pocket handkerchief, Elefante with his feistiness suggested that the old fire still burned within.

And much of his heat, as he sat in his office at 1508 Genesee St., was directed at those — newspapers, state investigators, political enemies — who he said ruined a good thing.

The good thing, he said, was the machine: It was simple and effective. It worked.

"Sure, it was simple," Elefante said. "Do a favor ... spend a buck."

"Rufie," as he is known to friend and foe, learned about money and politics, favors and connections early. At age 10, he was earning pocket money passing out cards for candidates at east Utica polling places.

Not too many years after that, Elefante lieutenants were the ones passing out the money. He recalled the scene in Marino's Restaurant — "little City Hall" — on election days.

"Say you had $100,000 to spend. You might give $300 to a campaign worker to help get out the vote in his ward."

If some of that money, unknown to the boss, ended up in constituents' pockets, well, "that was like paying the family, really. ... That's the political system. ... It's not illegal. ... That's the way it is."

Reformists might shudder, but Elefante maintains that the proof of such tactics was in the pudding. In his view, his way worked; the present system of more open and, by comparison, more fragmented and disorganized government, doesn't.

"My greatest accomplishment," he said, "is that everything that Utica's got, we brought to Utica, and nobody has brought anything since.

"My greatest regret is that we never got any credit for it. All I got was a bad rap by the news media."

The Elefante machine may have had its birth one day in 1928 on the corner of Bleecker and Mohawk streets on Utica's Italian east side. A young Franklin Delano Roosevelt was running for governor, and his swing through upstate cities, up to then, had been lackluster. Elefante helped turn out a crowd of 10,000 for a Utica rally.

See ELEFANTE, Page 6A

Veteran Observer-Dispatch staffer Michael J. Woods moves from the editorial page to take over coverage of Utica City Hall beginning today. In his first major assignment, Woods landed an exclusive interview with political power broker Rufus P. Elefante. In a recent hour-long interview at Elefante's office, the longtime political leader touched on subjects ranging from his childhood to his city's future.

WOODS

Rufus Elefante remembers

'RUFIE'

Through the years

For nearly a quarter century, the name Rufus P. Elefante has been closely associated with Utica politics. For more than two decades after World War II, Elefante was centrally involved in the decision-making process in the city. On this page is a pictorial look through the years at the man known simply as "Rufie." At far left, Elefante (left) is shown with former Utica Board of Water Supply Manager Dennis O'Dowd in the 1940s. In the top photo, an animated Elefante makes a point in an April 1974 meeting. Above are the changing faces of Rufus Elefante, in the late 1940s (left), in 1965 (center) and in 1986.

'My greatest accomplishment is that everythin that Utica's got, we brought to Utica, and nobody has brought anything since. My greatest regret i that we never got any credit for it. All I got was a

'Rufie,' a Utica legend, dies

From staff reports

Rufus P. (Rufie) Elefante, who lived and breathed politics in Utica for three quarters of a century, influencing almost every facet of community life with his behind-the-scenes power, died yesterday at the age of 91.

Elefante, who had been hospitalized for several months, died at 10:20 a.m. yat St. Luke's-Memorial Hospital Center.

"We've watched the passing of a living legend," said Rep. Sherwood Boehlert, R-23, who used to talk about politics with Elefante, after church on Sundays, at Uncle Henry's Pancake House where Elefante held court.

"I can look back at the time I spent with him and recall it was a history lesson.

RUFUS
ELEFANTE
1903 - 1994

"When he was at his prime, he was a significant force, not just in this area, but beyond."

Elefante was the last of the old-time political bosses. He never held elective office; never chaired a political party; never sat in a position of authority higher than a seat on the water board. Yet no one in this century had a more sustained impact on the area's politics, government, economy or sense of itself.

To his admirers, he was a civic-spirited political genius whose years of peak power in the 1930s, '40s and '50s were associated with the city's last great heyday. Whether it was finding a job for a friend, or befriending the area with industries and jobs, Rufie was the man who made things happen.

But to others, he represented political feudalism at its worst, using money, patronage and other favors to reward his soldiers, and to build a self-serving machine that hampered progress. In the eyes of his critics, he obstructed anything that didn't serve his own interests; his detractors characterized his reign as "rule or ruin."

Observer-Dispatch file photo

■ The long-time Democratic kingmaker is very hard to define. **Page 10A**

■ Elefante's influence in Utica was enormous and lasting. **Page 10A**

■ Friends and adversaries say Rufie was a man who loved his city. **Page 11A**

■ There never will be another politician like Rufus P. Elefante. **Page 11A**

■ In his last public interview in 1992, Elefante commented on many issues. **Page 11A**

11/16/94

Political leader hard to define

Rufus P. Elefante, the long-time Democratic kingmaker who died yesterday, defies definition.

A man who led a political machine that strangled progress and restricted power to the few, he was a master politician who single-handedly led the city's Italian-American population from being scorned and persecuted to having a lock on political power.

Russ Davis

He was a genius at the art of politics, but under his rule government was a mockery of democracy.

He was capable of incredible generosity to people in need but could also be merciless to those who he felt betrayed him.

Throw away simplicity when talking about Elefante. There are not enough colors in a painter's palette to capture the whole man.

Recall the times. When Elefante's power was at its zenith, there were hookers on many downtown corners. I know. I saw them as a kid. It was a golden age for a few and a tarnished time for many.

Recall the man. It was a summer day on Genesee Street near the old City Hall. I had met Mayor Frank Dulan earlier. He was appropriately pompous and disinterested in meeting a little kid.

Then Mom and I met Elefante. He squatted down to talk with me as if I were a real person. We talked baseball. He gave me a big laugh and a smile, shook my hand as if I were ready to vote and went his way.

I liked the man — knowing this was the same man who abused his power in such a way that I could see city crews shoveling the driveway of an aide and mowing the man's lawn.

A nice man. A bad time. A living contradiction.

Recall the system. I remember standing in Uncle Henry's Restaurant trying to get up the courage to ask for a city job, even though my parents warned me we did not know anyone.

Finally a man asked me what I wanted. When I told him, he asked me my name, went over to where Elefante was sitting and came right back, telling me — firmly but nicely — the city had no jobs. The next week, they hired 30 kids for the parks.

I knew then the man and the system were both evil. Then a family friend's father died. The man had no money for the funeral. Elefante — who pulled the strings to get the man his job — paid the bill.

Politics? Maybe. But he never asked the man to do a thing. The episode taught me another lesson in the many layers of Elefante.

Throw out absolutes. Reality is not black, not white, but gray.

Then I was his enemy, crossing swords with Elefante as a reporter. I recall an interview with him in the building that now houses the FDR Democratic Club. Seated in a throne-like red leather chair, he growled and answered every question with an aspersion at the O-D.

It was a contentious confrontation. Yet, beneath it all, he was aware that it was all part of the game — a game he played better than anyone else I have met.

I recall the last time I heard his voice. Elefante called to complain about an editorial on regionalization of the Utica Board of Water Supply. After a vintage tirade — the kind of oratory only a true old-time politician could deliver — he said: "You newspaper people just don't understand. Everything I ever did, it was because I love this city and I love these people."

Maybe. Maybe it started that way before it became power for power's sake. Maybe it started out good, but it went bad along the way.

The machine Elefante led hurt Utica — a city I love as much as I know he did. But the man's politics was one thing. The man was another. Elefante was a leader, a master at the art of politics and a man who prized loyalty above all else.

I fought his policies, but I still admired the man. I don't know if he was a good man. But I know he was a great one. He was a giant, the kind who comes along rarely.

We will debate his political legacy forever. But one thing needs no debate: There will never be another like him.

God bless, Rufie.

Russ Davis is special projects editor of the Observer-Dispatch.

To hallow the memory and bless the soul
and to implore God's tenderest blessings

Rufus Elefante
is hereby enrolled in the

Sacred Heart Spiritual Society

and will share in the daily Mass
and prayers offered for all
members of the Society.

At the request of:

Senator Alfonse D'Amato

Date: 11-14-94

So Testifies:

Fr Bob Hess

Reverend Robert Hess, Spiritual Director
Sacred Heart Spiritual Society
Walls, Mississippi

Bibliography

Abramson, Rudy, *Spanning the Century: The Life of W. Averell Harriman, 1891-1986*, New York: William Morrow and Company, Inc., 1992.

Bean, Philip A., "The Irish, the Italians, and Machine Politics, a Case Study: Utica, New York, (1870-1960), *Journal of Urban Studies*, 20(2), February 1994, 205-239.

__________, "Leftists, Ethnic Nationalism, and the Evolution of Italian-American Identity and Politics in Utica's *Colonia*," *New York History*, 87 (4), Fall 2006, 423-74.

__________, "Watchdogs of the State," *New York Archives*, 7 (1), Summer 2007, 24-28.

Beetle, David H., "Rendezvous with Rufe," *Observer-Dispatch*, June 18, 1949, June 26, 1949, and July 3, 1949.

Benedetto, Richard, *Politicians are People, Too*, Lanham, Maryland: University Press of America, 2006.

Bollettino dell'Emigrazione, Roma: Cooperativo Tipografico Manuzio, (13) 1908.

Ehrenhalt, Alan, *The United States of Ambition: Politicians, Power, and the Pursuit of Office*, New York: Random House, 1991.

Ellis, David M., *The Upper Mohawk Country*, Woodland Hills, California: Windsor Publications, 1982.

Moscow, Warren, *Politics in the Empire State*, New York: Alfred A. Knopf, 1948.

Nassar, Fred, William Lucy, and Dominick Assaro, *What Utica Needs*, Utica: Renaissance Publishing Company, 1965.

"Pancake House Politicking," *Attenzione*, November 1980, 72-73.

Reports of the Immigration Commission: Emigration Conditions in Europe, Washington: United States Government Printing Office, (12), 1911.

Smith, Richard Norton, *Thomas E. Dewey and His Times*, New York: Simon & Schuster, 1982.

Thomas, Alexander R., *In Gotham's Shadow: Globalization and Community Change in Central New York*, Albany: State University of New York Press, 2003.

Robert Hunter Williams, *Vice Squad*, New York: Thomas Y. Cromwell Company, 1973.

Witt, Stuart K., "The Democratic Party in Utica," master's thesis, Syracuse University, 1962.

Biographies

Philip Bean (BA Union College, MA Oxford University, PhD University of Rochester), Dean of Academic Affairs, Haverford College. Author of several articles on immigration and political history and "The Urban Colonists: Italian American Identity and Politics in Utica, New York," forthcoming from Syracuse University Press in 2010.

Eugene Paul Nassar (BA Kenyon College, MA Oxford University, PhD Cornell University) Prof. Emeritus, Utica College. Author and editor of many books, including a memoir of growing up in East Utica, "Wind of the Land," from Syracuse University Press.

Angela Elefante (BA Manhattanville College, MA Cornell University, PhD and LLD, Catholic University, Certificate of Advanced Studies in International Law from the Hague Court.) Author of articles in the *Hague Journal.* Member of the Bar and the State Court of Appeals, New York State. Director of Instructional Media, Utica City School System.